SpringerBriefs in Law

More information about this series at http://www.springer.com/series/10164

Christoph Herrmann · Corinna Dornacher

International and European Monetary Law

An Introduction

Springer

Christoph Herrmann
Faculty of Law
University of Passau
Passau
Germany

Corinna Dornacher
Faculty of Law
Ludwig Maximilian University of Munich
Munich
Germany

ISSN 2192-855X ISSN 2192-8568 (electronic)
SpringerBriefs in Law
ISBN 978-3-319-57641-1 ISBN 978-3-319-57642-8 (eBook)
DOI 10.1007/978-3-319-57642-8

Library of Congress Control Number: 2017938622

Printed on acid-free paper

This Springer imprint is published by Springer Nature
The registered company is Springer International Publishing AG
The registered company address is: Gewerbestrasse 11, 6330 Cham, Switzerland

Preface

Monetary law has long been dealt with by a small group of specialists only. Some legal scholars even claimed that there was no such thing as monetary *law*. Obviously, this is not true. The opposite statement by Georg F. Knapp at the beginning of the 20th century: "Money is a creature of law" comes closer to the truth. Modern monetary systems cannot exist nor be imagined absent a legal framework. This is particularly true when it comes to cross-border financial activity or monetary integration within international organizations such as the European Union. Yet, monetary law is no easily accessible field of law, nor is it treated in course curricula at university very frequently, despite its obvious relevance in recent times of crisis.

With the present introduction, we try offer a guide to studying monetary law, international and European, and make the complicated interplay between economics (and sometimes politics) on the one hand, and law on the other, more comprehensible. It is based on our own research and teaching experience of the past years. A somewhat longer version of the work is currently being used as the backbone for an online course of the Virtuelle Hochschule Bayern (vhb), a virtual university of the Free State of Bavaria, Germany (http://www.vhb.org/en/homepage/). The vhb thankfully permitted the publication of this work to make it more widely accessible.

We hope that expectations of our readers are met and appreciate feedback to christoph.herrmann@uni-passau.de and corinna.dornacher@jura.uni-muenchen.de.

Passau, Germany — Prof. Dr. Christoph Herrmann LL.M.
Munich, Germany — Corinna Dornacher
March 2017

Contents

Chapter 1
Interdisciplinary Introduction to Money and Currencies

For a comprehensive understanding of the legal principles constituting European and International Monetary Law it is necessary to focus first on the subject matter at hand: Money. Despite the term's universal and frequent usage, few outside the world of economic academics have probably taken the time to ponder what money actually is, how it evolved historically and how monetary systems and policy function today.

1.1 History of Money

1.1.1 What Is Money?

This relatively simple question proves to be rather complicated to answer and has been the subject of an ongoing academic debate in economic, social and legal theory. The origins of the debate enjoy respectable antiquity and include the works of Aristotle, as well as later the works of scholars such as Weber, Schumpeter, Keynes and Friedman. Generally, three different approaches as to what money is can be distinguished:

The most practical approach is probably taken by economists, briefly stating "Money is what money does!".[1] The nature of money is thereby defined by the functions attributed to it. Generally, three characteristic functions are recognised, albeit it is controversial which is the predominant one: Medium of exchange, unit of account and store of value. Therefore, all existing financial assets (cash, demand deposits etc.) that fulfil these three functions are economically considered to be money.

In social theory, on the other hand, the role of the general public is strongly emphasised, assuming that any commodity which is used as a means of exchange

[1] I.a. Spahn (2003, p. 1).

C. Herrmann and C. Dornacher, *International and European Monetary Law*, SpringerBriefs in Law, DOI 10.1007/978-3-319-57642-8_1

constitutes money. This assumption links the nature of money to a recurring social practice of giving/receiving commodities as payment/consideration.

Conversely, in legal theory, *Knapp* most famously stated that "money is a creature of law",[2] meaning that only those commodities constitute money, which are equipped with purchasing power by the State. Yet, there is no general legal definition of money. The legal terminology used is inconsistent and the meaning of the term money varies significantly in criminal, public and civil law.

With that in mind, it is reasonable to define the socio-economic phenomenon of money somewhat pre-legally in order to gain an idea of what money is or could be. Considering the monetary functions in modern economies—medium of exchange, unit of account and store of value—such a definition could be: "A transferable unit of account, which is universally accepted as consideration for goods or services".[3] Furthermore, the general recognition of commodities as means of payment largely depends on the following characteristics: scarcity (actual or controlled), countability, uniformity, durability, portability and broad acceptance.

Currency on the other hand is defined as the regulation (not necessarily by sovereign power) of a monetary system based on a unit of account, which is used as means of exchange within a certain community. The term currency is also commonly used to describe the unit used in an organised monetary system (cf. Art. 3 (4) Treaty on European Union (TEU)).

1.1.2 Historical Development of Money

The history of money and monetary systems can be described and conceived as an actual socio-economic and cultural phenomenon, tracing back as far as the origins of mankind. The development began with the use of specific preferred barter goods (cowry shells, cattle etc.) as common means of exchange and evolved through the creation of metal and coin money, book money, banknotes and paper money into nowadays widely-used electronic forms of money. It has been a constant process of dematerialisation, incipient with real commodities transforming over time into virtual units of account without any innate utility.

The initial development of money stems from the need of people to exchange goods and services. Conversely, fully self-sufficient people in terms of goods and services do not need money. But even in the early stages of mankind a division of labour existed, creating a need for exchange with others. Initially the problem was solved by direct barter—a burdensome practice of searching for suitable exchange partners. These impracticalities are thought to be the reason behind the emergence of common means of exchange. Though they differed regionally, the means of exchange were usually coveted specific barter goods with an innate utility, e.g.

[2]Knapp (1923, p. 1).

[3]Herrmann (2010, p. 78).

cowry shells, cattle etc. (means of exchange theory).[4] This means of exchange theory is not undisputed in academia. Other explanations of the origin of money include religious and cultural causes for the choice of certain barter goods as means of exchange, e.g. the sacral meaning of cattle or because of a combination of aesthetics and human craving for recognition (so-called swank money). Ultimately, there is no mono-causal explanation for the origin of money. It was a lengthy process, influenced by social, religious and economic factors.

Barter goods were subsequently replaced by precious metals, which proved to be the most popular means of exchange as they were scarce, countable, uniform, durable and portable in bars. But although the physical characteristics of metal predestined it as a means of exchange, it also caused problems. Before an exchange could be executed, the metal had to be weighed and counted and its quality had to be determined, which caused delays and disputes. In an attempt to solve this problem, coins were invented—pre-weighed standardised portions of a specific metal. Additionally, in order to certify the measurements, the coins were later on minted. In the Western World the birth of the metal coin dates back to 600–800 BC (possibly even earlier in China and India).[5] This marks both the beginning of the idea that money has its own character and functions abstract and distinct from the commodity used for exchange, and the beginning of the State influence on money. States quickly claimed the right of coinage as part of their sovereignty, hence taking the first step towards a monetary system and the creation of currencies. Throughout the span of the metal era, different metals were in use, mostly however silver and gold which led to the era of Bimetallism. The coexistence of both metals lasted until the end of the 19th century when gold became the single monetary standard. By this time, gold coins were not actually circulating anymore: ever since the 13th century, they had gradually been replaced by paper money and token coins, whose value was not determined by their metal content anymore. Token coins were merely a representation of silver and gold. Yet gold still played an important role as the value of the money depended on its relation to the gold reserves of the currency.

The triumph of paper money ensued due to the difficulties in transportation of larger amounts of metal and the occasionally insufficient availability of precious metal, which complicated matters further. Ever since the commercial revolution of the 13th century, merchants therefore began to issue drafts and bonds in writing, which could be converted into certain amounts of real metal. The merchant's metal was stored by a changer, who would convert the bonds and drafts for them. As the practice of cashless payment evolved, changers simultaneously assumed the role of bankers. The stored metal was technically book money, an early form of demand deposits. The changers additionally began to loan the metal of their deposits to other clients, which created a significant problem inherent to every financial system up until today: The collapse of a bank caused by its inability to issue cash, resulting

[4]For an overview see Davies (2016, pp. 10 ss, 35 ss).

[5]Davies (2016, pp. 57 ss).

from a run—a sudden and simultaneous withdrawal of money by bank clients—after a major fallout in its credit business.

The circulation of these papers increased and goldsmiths began to hand out receipts or goldsmith notes to clients, denominating the stock of gold stored. These notes were transferable by endorsement and also used and accepted as means of payment. Around 1670, London goldsmiths standardized the notes, pre-denominating smaller amounts of gold instead of the respective stock or the specific amount of gold used in a single transaction. Subsequently, goldsmith notes even became transferable without endorsement. Meanwhile other banks and even States started to issue such notes too. Legally, these notes were bonds payable to the bearer and transferable without endorsement. Due to their widespread public acceptance as direct form of payment, the notes (paper money) achieved monetary status for the first time and were rarely returned to their issuer. Yet our modern version of paper money only emerged and developed between the 18th and 20th century after the issuance and authorisation of banknotes were brought under national governments' control by securing a monopoly for public and some private central banks, granting paper money the status of legal tender and ending the gold/silver backing as well as the obligation to convert. Ultimately, this also marked the end of the metal era, not however the end of the process of monetary development.[6]

The final stage of this process of dematerialisation was reached with the beginning of the information age from 1950 onwards. The introduction of electronic payment transactions and electronic money (e-money) took dematerialisation one step further and presented a purely virtual form of money without any innate value. However, it is important to differentiate between electronic payment transactions and e-money, because they differ significantly. The former is simply an electronic and thus more effective version of the known and traditional book money instruments. The latter is a demand deposit, which is saved on data mediums, issued in exchange for (real) money and accepted by companies as means of payment (e.g. prepaid cards). The legal construction is similar to bearer bonds, although e-money naturally cannot be qualified as a certificate. Since e-money can only be used for a single payment transaction, ceases to exist after conversion into cash or book money and is completely dependent on national monetary systems and traditional banking services, it cannot be considered as virtual money just yet. A different assessment may be pertinent with regard to so-called "crypto-currencies"[7] or virtual currencies, a notable example being Bitcoins. Crypto-currencies rely on peer-to-peer networks, are thus decentralized, globally distributed and pseudonymous due to the encryption transactions.[8] In contrast to e-money, crypto or virtual currencies' funds are not expressed in traditional currency units (Euro, Dollar etc.)

[6]For a detailed study of the development see Davies (2016, pp. 183 ss).

[7]For further information on crypto-currencies see https://www.ecb.europa.eu/pub/pdf/other/virtualcurrencyschemesen.pdf.

[8]For information on the technological background and functioning of Bitcoins see: Simonite (2011), The Economist (2015).

but in the respective virtual accounting unit (e.g. Bitcoins).[9] Within the respective community, they fulfil monetary functions and some, Bitcoins in particular, are convertible into traditional currencies and have a free floating (thus far very volatile) exchange-rate. The ECB cautiously defined them as "*a digital representation of value, not issued by a central bank, credit institution or e-money institution, which in some circumstances can be used as an alternative to money*".[10] The careful choice of words and rather vague formulation hint at the still highly disputed monetary and legal status of crypto-currencies. The European Court of Justice (ECJ) recently implied in a preliminary ruling that Bitcoins are indeed to be classified as a currency, albeit a virtual one.[11] Other commentators,[12] however, regard the characterization as a virtual currency as a simplification of the technological and economic options offered by crypto-currencies. The ECB even rejects the idea of crypto-currencies being money or currencies in that sense altogether based on economic and legal considerations.[13] And the German Federal Financial Supervisory Authority decided to treat them as a form of private money falling under the general category of financial instruments, § 1 XI German Banking Act (KWG) for regulatory purposes.[14] This exemplifies that the issue of virtual money is far from being resolved and the aforementioned judgement most likely only marks the beginning rather than the end of the legal debate.

1.2 Monetary Policy Basics

1.2.1 Two-Tier Mixed Monetary System

With the exception of a few countries, which use a currency board system (foreign currency backing for the domestic currency), the two-tier mixed monetary system is universally employed. The two tiers of the system consist of central banks on the one hand and commercial banks on the other. The system is mixed because money is provided by central banks (monetary base or "high powered money") and by commercial banks (book or bank money). Both monetary forms are economically considered as money. The issuance of cash is normally a monopoly of central banks, which manage the supply of money. Commercial banks on the other hand can generate money by allowing demand deposits on credit in central bank money

[9]ECJ, judgement from October 22nd 2015, Skatteverket/Hedqvist, C-264/14, para. 12.

[10]ECB (2015, p. 4).

[11]ECJ, judgement from October 22nd 2015, Skatteverket/Hedqvist, C-264/14, para. 12 and 24.

[12]See e.g. Maupin (2015), http://voelkerrechtsblog.org/the-ecjs-first-bitcoin-decision-right-outcome-wrong-reasons/.

[13]ECB (2015, pp. 23 ss).

[14]BaFin (2014), https://www.bafin.de/SharedDocs/Veroeffentlichungen/EN/Fachartikel/2014/fa_bj_1401_bitcoins_en.html.

(banknotes or central bank book money), which generally does not enjoy the status of legal tender, but is regularly accepted as payment in commerce. Combined, the financial institutions generate the money in any given currency area. While central banks possess the ability of (theoretically) limitless creation of money (and also elimination of money by reselling e.g. bonds on the market), commercial banks often face a liquidity problem: Loans can ultimately only be repaid with central bank money, whose supply is limited by the central bank. The problem is similar to the one described above, resulting from the obligation to convert into gold or silver.

1.2.2 Monetary Aggregates

The amount of money in circulation is described using different monetary aggregates (M0, M1, M2, M3).[15] M0 describes the monetary base or high powered money (central bank money). In reality, commercial banks have developed an increasing number of financial products (assets), which fulfil more or less monetary functions (depending on their characteristics) and therefore exhibit varying degrees of "moneyness". Monetary aggregates reflect this by differing in terms of liquidity and included assets, from M1 (narrow) over M2 (intermediate) to M3 (broad). M3 is generally considered the best indicator for future developments in the overall level of prices, as it includes a wide range of financial assets. Coincidently, it is also the aggregate least affected by central bank influence.

The actual macroeconomic amount of money supplied is a product of M0 and a multiplier, which is determined by the central banks' minimum reserves policy and the preferred relation between cash and commercial bank money held by non-banks. Although this formula suggests absolute control by central banks over the supply of money (making it a quantity determined by exogenous factors), many argue that the activity of commercial banks has a significant influence, turning it into a quantity determined by endogenous factors in reality. The demand of money on the other hand is defined as the preferred cash management of non-banks. In this regard, money competes with other forms of storing value like bonds, immobile assets etc. whereby non-banks are assumed to have an affinity for liquidity. The short- and long-term stability of the monetary demand is highly debated among economists; so far, the empirical data is inconclusive in this respect.

1.2.3 Monetary Policy and Policy Instruments

Monetary policy itself is defined as the targeted exercise of influence on the supply of money in an economy by influencing monetary aggregates and interest rates in

[15]ECB (2011, p. 50).

order to achieve specific economic goals. Such goals generally are the stability of monetary value (as indicated by the level of prices), the pursuit of specific exchange-rates and economic stabilization policies. The interrelations of these goals are not free of conflict, usually prompting central banks to prioritize one or the other. Central banks have an array of instruments at hand to control/influence monetary processes. Among them are the creation of central bank money, determination of the central rate, minimum reserve obligations for commercial banks to limit their ability of generating money, and open market operations. An important task of monetary policy is to guarantee a sufficient supply of money in order to secure the liquidity of the banking sector, while at the same time setting limits for their refinancing options in order to prevent excessive spending activities, which would threaten financial markets and policy goals likewise.

1.2.4 Currencies

Money has an internal value, the purchasing power, and an external value, the exchange-rates. The exchange-rate is subject to the exchange-rate policy (technically a subchapter of monetary policy). The decisive parameters for the currency policy are the convertibility of the currency into foreign currencies and whether the exchange-rate is free floating or fixed. The differentiation of internal and external is somewhat artificial as exchange-rate policy decisions can affect the internal value of money as well. An increase of the exchange-rate, for example, reduces the inflationary tendencies, due to cheapened imports and a decrease in demand abroad for national products. Conversely, the purchase of the national currency by central banks in exchange for foreign currencies expands the amount of (national) money.

1.2.5 Monetary Policy and Fiscal Policy

Monetary and fiscal policy are linked as well. This link is most obvious when the "banknote press" is employed or when public budgets are directly financed with central bank money (monetisation of sovereign debt) as both measures directly expand the amount of money circulating and thus have inflationary effects.

1.3 Money and the Law

Initially, despite the works of some scholars, law was not considered to play an important role in the monetary sphere as theories of metallism and means of exchange dominated the conception of both the idea of money and its value. Yet, according to the state theory of *Knapp*, "money is a creature of law". In this absoluteness, money would only be conceivable in combination with a sovereign authority. Legal acts would be the defining force in monetary matters. But are they?

Firstly, the State theory did help to overcome the era of metallism and the idea that any monetary system needs to be backed by silver or gold and equipped with an obligation to convert in order to be stable and functioning. Also the monetary monopoly of States, which is almost invariably established by modern constitutional law, is effectively recognised as part of their sovereignty by international law (see Chap. 2). Furthermore, legal rules as well as the judiciary play an important role in economic and commercial life. But at the same time the State theory mistakes a natural and practical (State) monopoly for a natural right to define and control money. The validity of money depends largely on broad popular acceptance. People will only accept payment/consideration in money, because they expect other members of the same society will behave in the same manner. The acceptance, originally stemming from the appreciation of the substance used, is nowadays indeed based on a legal foundation: obligation to accept as payment, prohibition of other currencies, taxing authority of the State. The State's influence on acceptance, however, is ultimately limited. Legal definitions, for example, can only ever affect concrete forms of money, but are incapable—since it is simply impossible—of legally influencing the purchasing power of money by denomination. Moreover, even the law itself provides examples of a broader sense of the term money, e.g. § 35 of the German Bundesbank Act,[16] which clearly identifies other means of exchange different from the legal tender as money.

Ultimately, defining money as a creature of law amounts to disregarding the socio-economic dimension of money. Therefore, the State theory approach has subsequently been modified, in order to be able to explain real life developments such as non-acceptance of the legal tender. It has been argued that legal regulations concerning money could be altered by customary law. Others claimed that the refusal of acceptance does not merely affect the characterisation of money; rather, it deprives the underlying norm of its legal status altogether. *Hahn* and *Siebelt* on the other hand asserted a dual creation process for money, meaning that money depends on both law and social acceptance. Similarly, *Proctor* attributed to law the ability to abstractly define what money is, but found that the State lacks control over what is actually used as means of payment within the economy.

Another controversially discussed question is whether the obligation to accept the legal tender is at all a prerequisite for money. Two counterarguments should be considered: Firstly, this would limit the State's power to create a monetary system without such an obligation and secondly, foreign money would then automatically lose its monetary status, due to its lack of legal tender status abroad. However, foreign money is clearly regarded as money in legal norms such as § 146 of the

---

[16]An English version of the Bundesbank Act can be found at http://germanlawarchive.iuscomp.org/?p=833#35.

German Criminal Code.[17] The obligation to accept a legal tender is therefore more likely to have practical consequences when a competing means of exchange is circulating and a broader acceptance of the legal tender, which it has not achieved based on its value or quality, needs to be secured.

In summary, the State is free to define money through legal acts. This is part of the sovereignty of each State. However, law is more commonly used to regulate what already exists, rather than as a tool for invention. The aforementioned socio-economic phenomenon of money thus details what legally could be regarded as money; not what the law actually does recognise as money. This does not automatically render the State theory meaningless nor does it mean that law has no influence on money at all. A modern economy needs a functioning monetary system. A collapse would have severe consequences for the economy and the wellbeing of the population. It is therefore unlikely that a State will leave monetary issues solely to the social and economic market forces. Monetary regulations are necessary and play a dominant role today, for example in contract or public international law. Maybe the role of the State is best described as that of a company with a dominant market position, which protects the company's standard and market share (tax demands and public payments) with all available methods and consistently defies any competition.

References

BaFin (2014) Bitcoins: Supervisory assessment and risks to users. https://www.bafin.de/SharedDocs/Veroeffentlichungen/EN/Fachartikel/2014/fa_bj_1401_bitcoins_en.html

Davies G (2016) A history of money, 4th edn. University of Wales Press, Cardiff

ECB (2011) The monetary policy of the ECB 2011. https://www.ecb.europa.eu/pub/pdf/other/monetarypolicy2011en.pdf

ECB (2015) Virtual currency schemes—a further analysis. https://www.ecb.europa.eu/pub/pdf/other/virtualcurrencyschemesen.pdf

Herrmann C (2010) Währungshoheit, Währungsverfassung und subjektive Rechte. Mohr Siebeck, Thübingen

Knapp G (1923) Staatliche Theorie des Geldes, 4th edn. Duncker & Humblot, München

Maupin J (2015) The ECJ's first Bitcoin decision: right outcome, wrong reasons? http://voelkerrechtsblog.org/the-ecjs-first-bitcoin-decision-right-outcome-wrong-reasons/

Simonite T (2011) What Bitcoin is and why it matters. MIT Technology Review. http://www.technologyreview.com/news/424091/what-bitcoin-is-and-why-it-matters/

Spahn H-P (2003) Money as a social bookkeeping device. From mercantilism to general equilibrium theory

The Economist (2015) The trust machine. The economist. http://www.economist.com/news/leaders/21677198-technology-behind-bitcoin-could-transform-how-economy-works-trust-machine

[17] An English version of the Criminal Code can be found at http://germanlawarchive.iuscomp.org/?p=752.

Chapter 2
Monetary Sovereignty and History of International Monetary Law

2.1 Monetary Sovereignty under Public International Law

The aforementioned principle of monetary sovereignty plays an important role in monetary law and is key to understanding international monetary relations notwithstanding the much discussed potential erosion of the principle.

2.1.1 The General Principle of Sovereignty

Like the term money before the principle of sovereignty is not as easily accessible as the widespread use of the term in legal, political and economic discussions might suggest. The complexity stems on the one hand from the issues (legality, legitimacy and power) involved and on the other hand from sometimes varying understandings of the term in different academic fields.

2.1.1.1 Content of the Principle

The legal principle of sovereignty generally encompasses the supreme authority within a territory entrusted to the State as the political institution (internal dimension or sovereignty within the State) as well as its international independence from other States or from interference with its internal affairs (external dimension or sovereignty of the State) except for obligations under public international law. In a nutshell, sovereignty hence denotes a status of self-determination and independence.[1] Today, it is among the fundamental principles of public international law

[1]See also M. Huber in Island of Palma Case (Netherlands vs. USA), 1928, 2 UNRIAA 829.

C. Herrmann and C. Dornacher, *International and European Monetary Law*,
SpringerBriefs in Law, DOI 10.1007/978-3-319-57642-8_2

and considered to be one of the guiding concepts of international relations (cf. Art. 2 (1) Charter of the United Nations).

2.1.1.2 Historical and Theoretical Development of the Principle

Historically, the modern concept of sovereignty is closely linked to the evolution of the nation state in Europe. Thus, the Peace of Westphalia in 1648,[2] ending the Thirty Years' War, is often cited as the starting point of a system of sovereign States. Against the backdrop of medieval (often religiously motivated) struggles for power and competence between clergy, nobility, classes and cities, a unifying authority was regarded as the only potential safeguard to establish and preserve peace and order.[3] It is not surprising therefore that *Jean Bodin*[4] developed the idea of a State equipped with absolute and lasting force, which is only subject to God's or nature's law, certain general legal principles and contracts the respective State has entered into.[5] Internally, the most important development in the conception of sovereignty and its origins was the change from sovereignty of the monarch (*Bodin, Hobbes, Machiavelli*) to sovereignty of the people (*Locke, Montesquieu, Rousseau*). Consequently, the State was (and still is) understood as an aggregate of individuals, who are the original sovereignty-holders, representing and exercising their collective will through its (constitutionally prescribed, elected) bodies. Externally, the removal of the personal link between sovereignty and monarch was facilitated by the perception of the State as a judicial entity. The judicial entity "State" could replace the monarch, a natural person, as the bearer of sovereign rights. Thus, sovereignty of the State and not only within the State became possible. Today, voices in academic and popular literature predicting the steady erosion or at least a significant alteration of the principle due to constraints caused by economic globalization and increasingly integrated financial markets worldwide are becoming louder. Specifically with regard to Greece and Argentina the issue of sovereignty infringements has been raised. Let it suffice here to note that the exercise of sovereignty has never been absolute but always depended on what was possible in reality. Therefore it seems reasonable to separate legal from political sovereignty, the latter often being more a question of power rather than legal rights and subject to constant change.[6]

---

[2]http://www.britannica.com/event/Peace-of-Westphalia.

[3]See for example: Fowler and Bunck (1995, pp. 4 s), Herrmann (2010, p. 90).

[4]www.constitution.org/bodin/bodin.txt.

[5]Before, the adjective "sovereign" was used mainly in legal procedure terminology to signify the non-appealability of last instance court decisions. For a more detailed overview of the philosophical development see Lastra (2015, pp. 6 ss).

[6]Herrmann (2010, p. 92 ss).

In summary, by its very nature as an abstract concept, sovereignty has on some occasions shaped political reality but often also merely retraced that reality, integrating it into a legal framework.

2.1.2 Monetary Sovereignty

"It is indeed a generally accepted principle that a state is entitled to regulate its own currency."[7]

Monetary sovereignty is part of a State's sovereignty and signifies the power to issue and regulate money within a specified territory. The above statement by the Permanent Court of International Justice is often cited as authority for the existence of monetary sovereignty for lack of an express recognition or definition in the Charter of the United Nations (UN) or the IMF Articles of Agreement. *Proctor* even places money among the prima facie matters of a State.[8] This is particularly interesting since monetary matters were by no means originally State matters as outlined in Chap. 1. Rather, States have successfully taken over monetary matters due to some practical advantages they have compared to private entities. It was only afterwards that philosophers and jurists fortified the existing exercise of the right with theoretical reasoning and integrated it into a coherent legal framework.[9] The wording of the judgment, in particular, suggests a customary legal nature of monetary sovereignty, indicating that the concept is potentially dynamic as it depends on a generally accepted practice.[10]

2.1.2.1 Content

Monetary sovereignty resides with the nation State and not with central banks despite their prominent role in monetary matters. The right encompasses the power to issue a currency (lex monetae/ius cudendae monetae), to regulate money, to control monetary policy, to control the exchange-rate policy and to impose exchange and capital controls.[11] It follows from this that States must generally recognize monetary legal acts of other States, which is especially important in contract law (currency changeover).[12] One particular side effect of this rule of

[7]www.icj-cij.org/pcij/serie_A/A_20/62_Emprunts_Serbes_Arret.pdf, http://www.icj-cij.org/pcij/serie_A/A_20/62_Emprunts_Bresiliens_Arret.pdf.

[8]Proctor (2012, p. 526).

[9]Zimmermann (2013, p. 9).

[10]Similarly Lastra (2015, p. 18).

[11]Lastra (2015, p. 19), Proctor (2012, pp. 500 s, 526 s).

[12]For a more detailed analysis of the recognition of the exercise of specific aspects of monetary sovereignty see Proctor (2012, pp. 526 ss).

international law is the phenomenon known as currency war: States seeking to secure an economic advantage by manipulating the value of their currencies. The manipulation can occur in three ways: (1) inflexible pegs of undervalued currencies; (2) resisting a currency appreciation in a floating exchange-rate regime and (3) quantitative easing.[13] Especially China has been accused of such tactics in past years.[14] There is no ground for impugning such measures in general international law, since they constitute a direct exercise of sovereign rights. Yet, they may violate certain obligations under the IMF Articles of Agreements (see Chap. 5).

2.1.2.2 Erosion of the Principle

Nevertheless, the monetary monopoly of the State has been questioned in recent years with some arguing that it is on the verge of erosion due to voluntary surrender but also due to limitations caused by globalization, information technology and economic and financial developments in the past decades.[15]

A prominent example of a voluntary surrender is the European Monetary Union (EMU). The transfer of specific sovereign powers to the European Union (EU) has been understood to erode or at least limit the sovereignty of individual Member States. In terms of competences, this assessment might be accurate; Member States of EMU are, for example, no longer competent to set a monetary policy. Another argument often brought forward to this end is the irrevocability of the EMU, since no exit provision exists in the Treaties apart from Art. 50 Treaty on European Union (TEU), which allows Member States to leave the EU altogether.[16] Yet rather than focusing on matters of competence or power it is noteworthy that a voluntary transfer of sovereign rights in accordance with international law constitutes one form of exercising such sovereign powers and not an infringement of them. Thus, *Zimmermann* convincingly considers the EMU a "joint exercise" or "a form of cooperative sovereignty" rather than a limitation or erosion.[17] With regard to the IMF, mainly its role during the financial crisis has been criticized, the allegation being that it exerts too much influence by making financial assistance conditional on ever more specific structural reforms and therefore practically determining a variety of domestic policies.[18] This again is an allegation based on factual

---

[13]Pisani-Ferry and Darvas (2010, p. 3).

[14]For a detailed analysis of China see Garcia-Herrero (2015).

[15]Lastra (2015, p. 20); Considering the participation in the EMU to be a limitation of sovereignty see also Treves (2000, p. 116).

[16]It is disputed among commentators whether it is indeed impossible for a Member State to leave the EMU but not the EU. See https://www.ecb.europa.eu/pub/pdf/scplps/ecblwp10.pdf. Additionally, the "irrevocability" wording of the Maastricht Treaty was eliminated by the Lisbon Treaty (see Art. 119 II TFEU) and even originally did not address the Member States as 'masters of the treaties' but referred to secondary law and thus addressed EU or formerly EC institutions.

[17]Zimmermann (2013, p. 143 s); see also Mabbett and Schelkle (2014).

[18]See Lowenfeld (2002, p. 257).

developments or power considerations and not a de jure situation reflected in the IMF Agreement, which actually reasserted national sovereignty with the second Amendment in 1978. Globalization and so called "private money" are frequently cited as threats to monetary sovereignty as well. In this context, globalization refers to the "deterritorialization" of money which stands in contrast to the territorial link of national sovereignty.[19] Control over the currency ultimately diminishes when it circulates globally and escapes the confinement of national borders. Private money (substitute, parallel or virtual currency) on the other hand will start circulating if the acceptance of the legal tender declines or vanishes completely. Both phenomena, however, again rather exemplify a weakened effect/success of national monetary policy or regulation not a loss of the sovereign right itself.

At the outset, monetary sovereignty was identified as a dynamic concept. Hence the legal principle can theoretically be altered by factual changes. Time, State practice and acceptance are the key requirements to alter a customary legal principle. There is no evidence that any of the alleged threats indeed fulfills these requirements, especially regarding the latest re-nationalization developments some financial markets and institutions are experiencing in the aftermath of the financial crisis.

2.2 History of International Monetary Law

Before 1944, there was practically no international monetary law. The gold standard, which had evolved during the 19th century, functioned without any legally binding regulation at international level and up until the World War I monetary and capital flight were hardly limited.

2.2.1 Gold Standard

The international gold standard was a monetary understanding amongst the major countries to use gold as the main reserve asset. As outlined in Chap. 1, the gold standard started with the end of bimetallism, which was brought about when most countries gradually opted for gold instead of other precious metals as a reserve asset. England was the first in 1717 and as others followed gold was universally used by 1870.[20] The gold standard lasted until 1914. The underlying understanding was that each participating country would guarantee the free convertibility of its currency into gold at a fixed price. This, of course, facilitated the free convertibility

---

[19]See Cohen (2000, p. 1).

[20]Davies (2016, p. 357).

of each currency into all other currencies at a fixed price.[21] The understanding, however, was not based on a formal international agreement and thus did not impose any international legal obligation upon the countries adopting the gold standard.[22] As the name indicates, gold was the system's core. The value of currencies was fixed against gold by the countries and the central banks held gold in their reserves to defend/back up that fixed price (so called "pure" gold standard).[23] Even before World War I some countries were already on a so-called gold-exchange standard, meaning that their central banks did not or not entirely hold reserves in gold, but also currencies of countries whose reserves consisted entirely of gold. At the time, the preferred (reserve) currency was Sterling, after World War II under Bretton Woods (for details see below) it was the US Dollar.

2.2.2 *The Creation of the Bank for International Settlements (BIS)*

The acrimonious atmosphere after World War I thwarted all attempts to focus on reestablishing peace and prosperity. Instead, the Treaty of Versailles of 29 June 1919 imposed reparation payments on Germany (and its allies) and a universal reintroduction of a system similar to the gold standard failed. Even though some countries adopted certain features of the gold standard unilaterally between 1925 and 1931, the system was entirely abandoned in 1931. The issue of reparations was first addressed by the Dawes Plan and later by the Young Plan.[24] In the context of the latter, the Bank for International Settlements (BIS)[25] was established in 1930 to administer German reparation payments (a task previously performed by the Agent General for Reparations in Berlin) and to serve as a trustee for the Dawes and Young Loans (to finance reparations). Further objectives of the BIS included the promotion of central bank cooperation and financial assistance (cf. Art. 3 Statutes of the BIS). At the time the relevance of the BIS was soon undermined though by the end of reparations in 1933/34, the breakdown of the gold standard and the attitude of most countries (see below).[26] The Bretton Woods conference even called for its liquidation in the Final Act of the conference, opting to create a new institution over reviving the existing one. Ultimately, the liquidation plan was never put into action and the BIS has indeed developed into a center for central bank cooperation and

---

[21]Davies (2016, p. 357).

[22]Lastra (2015, p. 409).

[23]Lastra (2015, pp. 409 s).

[24]Named after an American Banker O. Young, who presided over a Committee of Experts to resolve the issue of German reparations.

[25]For a detailed study of the history of the BIS see Toniolo (2005, Chap. 2 ss).

[26]Lastra (2015, p. 411).

institutional home for a variety of committees dealing with international financial standards.[27]

2.2.3 The Establishment of the IMF

The Articles of Agreement of the IMF were adopted on 22 July 1944 by 44 of 45 member states (the Soviet Union never became a signatory) participating in the International Monetary and Financial Conference of the United and Associated Nations taking place in Bretton Woods, New Hampshire (commonly referred to as Bretton Woods).[28] The narrative of Bretton Woods, which consists of three pillars: the IMF, the International Bank for Reconstruction and Development (IBRD,[29] better known as World Bank) and International Trade Organization [ITO, never came into existence, now World Trade Organization (WTO)],[30] was to win the peace and learn from past experience.[31]

The inter-war period namely was marked by tensions, instability and economic problems (the Great Depression with worldwide effects[32]; high reparations, onerous war debt and high unemployment specifically in the case of Germany). It is widely believed that the economic problems in particular were a significant contributing factor in the breakdown of the peace.[33] There were initiatives to find cooperative solutions on an international level to tackle the effects of the depression and restore stability (cf. the London International and Monetary Conference 1933[34] or the objectives of the BIS). This aim was never achieved though as international economic collaboration collapsed against the backdrop of severe economic and political tensions,[35] which destabilized democratic regimes not only in Germany and heralded a phase of external policies driven purely by national considerations.

The establishment of the Bretton Woods system was a milestone in international monetary law since it was the first international legal system governing monetary relations. The IMF Articles of Agreement, entering into force on 27 December 1945, imposed legal obligations on member states for the first time. Despite changes to the Agreement (see below), it continues to be the basis for international economic governance in monetary matters. The initial purpose of the IMF was to

---

[27]Lastra (2015, pp. 414 s).

[28]Today the IMF has 189 members, http://www.imf.org/external/about.htm.

[29]The task of the IBRD was meant to be the facilitation of post-war reconstruction, though in the end the Marshall Plan proved to play the key role in that regard.

[30]This reflects the three dimensions of economic relations: Money, Investment and Trade.

[31]The expression goes back to Keynes (1919).

[32]For a detailed study see Friedman and Schwartz (1965).

[33]For a detailed outline of the inter-war period see Lastra (2015, p. 410 ss).

[34]Toniolo (2005, pp. 144–149).

[35]E.g. Industrial production dropped by 47% in the USA between 1929 and 1932.

foster cooperation and reconstruction after World War II in order to avoid repetition of the disastrous consequences resulting from economic policies adopted during the inter-war period by establishing an open and non-discriminatory international monetary system, a system of convertibility, exchange-rate stability and avoidance of restrictions on current payments.[36] Largely, it can be viewed as a means to stabilize international economic relations and cooperation in order to contribute to the preservation of peace. Other commentators argue that it also marked the beginning of the Cold War due to the Soviet Union not signing the agreement.[37]

2.2.4 *The IMF's Development*

The IMF, also known as the Fund, evolved significantly over the course of its existence, trying to adapt to the challenges it faced during the 70 years it played a part in shaping the global economy. Likewise, the legal basis, the Articles of Agreement, was amended and changed over time. The seven decades can be roughly divided into five periods: Cooperation and Reconstruction (1944–71); the end of the Bretton Woods regime (1972–81); Debt and painful reforms (1982–89); Societal Changes for Eastern Europe and Asian Upheaval (1990–2004); Globalization and the Crisis (2004–today).[38]

2.2.4.1 The Collapse of the Par Value System

The first milestone marking a change in the working of international monetary relations was the collapse of the par value system (also known as Bretton Woods regime). Under the original Articles of Agreement, a par value system was introduced, which could be described as a gold-dollar standard. The value of each member's currency was either defined in gold or in US Dollar, which had a fixed gold value [see Art. IV sec. 1 (a)]. The convertibility of the Dollar into gold at the fixed price was guaranteed by US monetary authorities. Participating members on the other hand were obliged to convert their currency into Dollars at a fixed price (official exchange-rate or parity rate). Theoretically, the original Articles of Agreement offered the possibility of adjusting the par value under certain circumstances (Art. IV sec. 5 (a) and 7). Initially the system seemed to offer predictability and stability of international monetary relations while creating a clear-cut mandate for the IMF to enforce adjustment rules and provide temporary resources in order to deal with short-term balance of payments problems. However, the par

[36]See http://www.imf.org/external/about/whatwedo.htm#key.

[37]James (1996, p. 70).

[38]See http://www.imf.org/external/about.htm.

value system suffered from a decisive problem, referred to as the Triffin dilemma.[39] At the core of the dilemma lies the ultimately limited supply of gold. A growing world economy implies an increase in demand for Dollar reserves. If these demands were to be accommodated, the Dollar/gold ratio would increase too, meaning that the fixed price will not represent the actual value of the Dollar anymore. This would lead to a decline in confidence in the US' ability to convert the Dollar into gold and consequently cause a rush to convert existing Dollar reserves, ultimately forcing the collapse of the system. If the demands were not to be accommodated, the world economy would likely succumb to deflation.

Already in the early 1960s it became apparent that the gold reserves were insufficient. Countermeasures by the central banks of the US, UK, Belgium, France, Netherlands, Germany, Italy and Switzerland included the creation of a "gold pool". Yet the parallel existence of private gold markets rendered it extremely difficult to keep the gold price stable. The ensuing abandonment of the gold pool project enabled the private gold price to be determined through supply and demand, triggering a rise of the gold price. The IMF tried to meet foreseeable liquidity problems by creating a supplementary exchange reserve asset, defined and maintained by the IMF: the Special Drawing Rights (SDR).[40] As the gold price continued to rise, even this measure proved to be insufficient. The US was forced to suspend the convertibility of Dollars into gold.[41] Another contributor to the collapse was that the adjustment "tools" foreseen in the original Articles of Agreement were not used due to political reasons. Attempts to repair the collapsed system failed. What resulted from the collapse was a de facto adoption of free floating exchange-rates in contrast to the fixed exchange-rates in operation before.[42]

2.2.4.2 Second Amendment to the IMF Articles of Agreement

The Second Amendment (1978) to the IMF Articles of Agreement introduced two major changes. Firstly, it officially permitted what was already common practice amongst member States: floating exchange-rates. Secondly, it transformed the role of the IMF. In the absence of substantive legal regulations permitting the Fund to control the exchange-rate arrangements of its members, the emphasis shifted from a primarily monetary one to a financial one, taking on issues such as supervising banking and capital markets, financial reform and debt restructuring in line with the broad objectives of the IMF, Art. I of the Articles of Agreement.[43] Surveillance became the Fund's central task. Originally this shift could probably be regarded as a

[39]Triffin (1960).

[40]See http://www.imf.org/external/np/exr/facts/sdr.htm.

[41]President Nixon formally declared the abandonment of the commitment to convert on 15 August 1971.

[42]For a detailed outline of developments after the collapse see Lastra (2015, p. 420 ss).

[43]Lastra (2015, p. 432).

decline in power for the Fund. During times of financial crisis and sovereign debt restructuring/crisis, however, the IMF has played a key role in the past and continues to do so: 1980s sovereign debt restructuring of less developed countries (LDC); 1990s transition to market economies of formerly communist countries/financial crises; 2007–today global financial crisis and Euro area sovereign debt crisis. These situations proved that when members are dependent on immediate financial assistance, surveillance, risk assessment and decisions of the IMF become rather powerful (perhaps too powerful, as some argue) tools despite the lack of substantive enforcement provisions in the Agreement.

2.2.4.3 Further Amendments

In order to enter into force, an Amendment to the IMF Articles of Agreement requires positive acceptance by three fifths of IMF members (currently 113 of the 189 members), representing 85% of the IMF's total voting power. Several further Amendments have been proposed and are awaiting acceptance, others have yet to enter into force.[44] Today, the three main functions of the IMF are: surveillance, financial and technical assistance.[45] The IMF itself seems to seek a more enhanced role in promoting global stability by expanding its mandate in particular with regard to financial sector issues. Thereby, the IMF is of the opinion that the current legal framework offers enough flexibility and allows for a broader interpretation which is still in line with the Vienna Convention of the Law of Treaties, Art. 31–32. This reasoning has to be seen within the context, however, that going through the amendment procedure in order to expressly expand the IMF's mandate would be a difficult task with an incalculable outcome.

References

Cohen B (2000) Life at the top: international currencies in the twenty- first century, Princeton University essays in international economics No. 221. Princeton University Press, Princeton

Fowler M, Bunck J (1995) Law and power and the Sovereign State. Penn State University Press, State College

Friedman M, Schwartz A (1965) The great contraction 1929–1933. Princeton University Press, Princeton

Garcia-Herrero A (2015) Internationalizing the currency while leveraging massively: the case of China. Bruegel, Brussels. http://bruegel.org/wp-content/uploads/2015/10/wp-15-121.pdf

Herrmann C (2010) Währungshoheit, Währungsverfassung und subjektive Rechte. Mohr Siebeck, Thübingen

---

[44]Information on the current status of Amendments can be found here: https://www.imf.org/external/np/sec/misc/consents.htm.

[45]See http://www.imf.org/external/np/exr/facts/glance.htm.

James H (1996) International monetary cooperation since Bretton Woods. IMF, Washington and Oxford University Press, Oxford

Keynes J (1919) The economic consequences of the peace, 1st edn. Macmillan & Co., Limited, London

Lastra R (2015) International financial and monetary law, 2nd edn. Oxford University Press, Oxford

Loewenfeld A (2002) The international monetary system and the erosion of sovereignty. Boston Coll Int Comp Law Rev 25:257–272

Mabbett D, Schelkle W (2014) The lack of monetary sovereignty is not the reason Eurozone countries struggled during the crisis. London School of economics and political science.http://blogs.lse.ac.uk/europpblog/2014/04/03/the-lack-of-monetary-sovereignty-is-not-the-reason-Euroarea-countries-struggled-during-the-crisis/

Pisani-Ferry J, Darvas Z (2010) The threat of currency wars. Bruegel, Brussels. http://bruegel.org/wpcontent/uploads/imported/publications/101130_ep_jpf_zd_The_threat_of_currency_wars_a_European_perspective_01.pdf

Proctor C (2012) Mann on the legal aspect of money, 7th edn. Oxford University Press, Oxford

Toniolo G (2005) Central Bank co-operation at the bank for international settlements, 1st edn. Cambridge University Press, Cambridge

Treves T (2000) Monetary sovereignty today. In: M. Giovanoli (ed) International monetary law. Oxford University Press, Oxford, pp 110–120

Triffin R (1960) Gold and the dollar crisis. Yale University Press, New Haven

Zimmermann C (2013) A contemporary concept of monetary sovereignty, 1st edn. Oxford University Press, Oxford

Davies G (2016) A history of money, 4th edn. University of Wales Press, Cardiff

Chapter 3
Fundamental Legal Problems of International Monetary Relations

3.1 Lack of a Universal Currency

Monetary sovereignty and thus monetary systems continue to be a primarily national matter. Their origin is a national one, confined to a specific territory. With the exception of monetary unions, every State issues its own currency and monetary regulations or decides to use a foreign currency for its own purposes. Therefore there is no universally valid and accepted means of payment—no universal currency.

The so-called "international currencies" or "vehicle currencies" are not to be mistaken for de facto universal currencies. They are simply currencies which are predominant in international trade and capital transactions due to the issuing State being a major force in international trade and a significant source of capital. Additionally, vehicle or international currencies usually feature certain characteristics such as being relatively stable in value, convertible, issued by a State with a stable political background and liberalized financial markets.[1] The most prominent example is the US Dollar,[2] but the Pound Sterling as well as the Euro, Japanese Yen and Swiss Franc have to varying degrees and at different times also served as international currencies. Recently, the Chinese Yuan has further gained in importance and closed the gap on the world's major currencies which is reflected by the IMF decision to include the Yuan in the SDR currency basket.[3] These currencies fulfill a dual function: They are national currencies and simultaneously global currencies of choice.

A "reserve currency" on the other hand is a foreign currency held by countries (often by their central banks) as a means to pay off international debt obligations or to influence their domestic exchange-rate. A common feature of becoming a reserve currency is usually that these currencies already serve as international or vehicle

[1] Lastra (2015, p. 421 s).
[2] See Goldberg (2010), Kenen (1983).
[3] See https://www.imf.org/external/np/sec/pr/2015/pr15540.htm.

C. Herrmann and C. Dornacher, *International and European Monetary Law*, SpringerBriefs in Law, DOI 10.1007/978-3-319-57642-8_3

currencies and thus lend itself easily to function as reserves.[4] Being the issuer of a reserve currency has both advantages and shortcomings: It enables the respective states to acquire investments abroad with their own currency but also regularly coincides for them with consistently running large balance of payment deficits.[5]

The globally distributed and decentralized "crypto-currencies" do not yet enjoy a sufficiently widespread acceptance as means of payment (see Chap. 1). Additionally, it is questionable whether States would ever be prepared to surrender monetary sovereignty in its entirety (the idea of crypto-currencies is ultimately to denationalize money[6]).

Thus the main issue remains unresolved: Payment and investment flows across borders affect at least two different monetary systems. The ensuing problems are: (1) Convertibility of currencies, (2) free movement of capital and payments, (3) choice/establishment of an exchange-rate regime and lastly (4) providing adequate international liquidity.

3.2 Convertibility

The characterization of a currency as convertible or inconvertible used to depend on the existence of a gold or other metallic standard, paper money being convertible into gold or other metals.[7] Today, after the demise of the gold standard and with regard to cross border payment flows, convertibility of a currency means the ability to exchange domestic currency for foreign currency and to use foreign currency for transactions.[8] A prerequisite for convertibility therefore is that States refrain from restricting or prohibiting the making or receipt of cross border payments and allow the exchange of domestic for foreign currency (and vice versa) for these purposes.

In economics, convertibility is a generic term encompassing capital and current account convertibility.[9] Capital account convertibility refers to the free movement of capital as will be further discussed below. Current account convertibility on the other hand means free movement of payments to conduct trade in goods and services.[10] Full convertibility is thus technically only achieved if capital and current accounts are both freely convertible, i.e. unrestricted access to exchange is available. Legal terminology deviates slightly from this understanding and regularly refers to free movement of payments only when using the term convertibility,

[4]Polak (1992, p. 340).

[5]For an overview see Polak (1992, pp. 339–342).

[6]Lerch (2015, p. 203).

[7]Proctor (2012, p. 73 s).

[8]Galbis (1996, p. 3).

[9]On the distinction between capital and current accounts see IMF (2008, p. 74).

[10]For a definition of current accounts see as well IMF (2008, p. 11).

treating the issue of capital mobility as a separate category.[11] Irrespective of the terminology used, the convertibility of a currency is always a matter of degree depending on the intensity and number of implemented restrictions.[12] The measures can range from restricting payments for imports (e.g. advance import deposit and margin requirements) and generally limiting the availability and use of foreign exchange to taxation of transactions and payments of invisibles (trade of non-tangible assets e.g. consulting services).[13] The motivation behind the implementation of such measures are often attempts to gain a competitive advantage or protectionist movements.

3.3 Exchange-Rate Systems

The convertibility of a currency also requires an exchange-rate system which determines the technicalities of the currency conversion. An exchange-rate expresses the price of one currency in terms of another and therefore primarily relates to a currency's external value rather than its domestic purchasing power.[14] When designing such an exchange-rate system, there are several options, but they can generally be distinguished as either flexible/free floating according to market forces or fixed/pegged by official (government controlled) rules.[15] Within these quite broad categories States can adapt a regime according to their specific needs or policy preferences in a variety of ways:

- Free floating, manage a float or floating with a specified exchange value/exchange-rate zone target (for rates to really float naturally both—domestic and foreign—exchange-rates must be floating)
- Pegging: The exchange-rate is fixed against either a single currency (anchor currency) or a currency basket
- "Crawling" peg, i.e. a systematic adjustment of the fixed exchange-rate according to a previously specified scheme
- Currency board: A monetary authority assigned to issue a domestic currency which is backed up by a foreign reserve currency combined with the legal obligation to convert the domestic currency into the foreign reserve currency on demand[16]
- "Dollarization", i.e. substituting the domestic currency with a foreign currency
- Currency Union.[17]

---

[11]See for example the terminology in the IMF Articles of Agreement, Art. VIII, section 2.

[12]For a detailed analysis of existing measures restricting convertibility see: IMF (2014, p. 31 ss).

[13]See IMF (2014, p. 34 s).

[14]Proctor (2012, p. 84 s).

[15]Lastra (2015, p. 425).

[16]For a detailed discussion of currency boards see: Lastra (2015, p. 103 ss).

[17]Herrmann (2007, p. 7 s), Lastra (2015, p. 425).

This model kit full of options shows that the classification as fixed or flexible—as practical as it is—can also be somewhat misleading: Floating rates may be managed to range around a desired, relatively "fixed" level and, conversely, pegs may be altered so frequently that the rate almost resembles a floating one.[18] Thus, in reality characterizations of fixed and free floating are again a matter of degree and not of absolutes.[19] Regardless of the chosen regime, however, all exchange-rates are in one way or another subject to fluctuations. Depending on the system, these alterations are either brought about by market forces (appreciation or depreciation of the currency in relation to other currencies) or officially imposed by the respective authority (devaluation or revaluation).[20]

The advantages and drawbacks of the decision for either fixed or flexible regimes are vehemently debated in economic literature and no clear-cut answer can be given. In the past, pegging has often been used as a policy tool of stabilization ("import of monetary stability"[21]), a notable example being the Bretton Woods regime, and continues to be employed in that way. Proponents of flexible exchange-rates usually emphasize the higher degree of internal monetary policy independence it offers as well as the "shock-absorber" function of flexible rates which allow for easier adjustments.[22]

3.4 Free Movement of Capital

In its broadest sense, free capital mobility is only fully achieved if States refrain from any regulatory or other measures which would impede foreign direct investment, (cross border) real estate investments or purchases, securities investments, granting of loans or credits and other operations with financial institutions.[23] In the context of convertibility of currencies this naturally requires (a) the unrestricted ability to convert domestic currency into foreign currencies for capital transactions and (b) the unrestricted use of domestic currency in international financial transactions.[24] Ideally, the global introduction of free capital mobility across borders would lead to an optimal allocation of resources and promote risk diversification. In practice the effects may be more adverse though if the macroeconomic framework is insufficiently developed and/or the financial sector weak, because capital flows

[18]Gold (1976, p. 8).

[19]Different view: Cross (1994).

[20]Proctor (2012, p. 84 s and 530ss).

[21]Herrmann (2007, p. 10).

[22]Herrmann (2007, p. 10 s); A list of all current regimes used by IMF Member States can be found here: https://www.imf.org/external/pubs/nft/2014/areaers/ar2014.pdf.

[23]IMF (2012, p. 8); and for a definition of capital flows see: http://ec.europa.eu/finance/capital/overview_en.htm.

[24]IMF (2012, p. 8).

are often volatile and can be relatively large in comparison to the size of the respective financial sector or a country's GDP. Historically the free movement of capital has been perceived very critically with both *White* and *Keynes* advocating the need for capital controls. Conversely, the present global trend—despite a slow-down triggered by the recent financial crisis—continues to move towards liberalizing capital flows as it is already the norm in most developed countries.[25]

3.5 International Liquidity

The adequacy of international liquidity represents a more fundamental issue resulting from monetary flows and increasing demand for money due to an expanding volume of international trade and payments. International liquidity is synonymous with reserves held by and available to individual countries to finance potential balance of payment deficits.[26] Assets capable of serving as reserves are defined by the IMF as "those external assets that are readily available to and controlled by monetary authorities for meeting balance of payment financing needs, for intervention in exchange markets to affect the currency exchange-rate and for other purposes [such as maintaining confidence in the currency and the economy (…)]".[27] Historically the primary reserve asset was gold followed by reserve currencies like the Dollar or Pound Sterling (which were themselves convertible into gold). Since the demise of the gold standard and the subsequent breakdown of the par-value system reserve assets diversified and individual countries' reserves are now comprised of a mix of different resources: gold reserves with central banks or the IMF, foreign exchange reserves (Dollar, Pound Sterling, Euro, Yen, Swiss Franc and Yuan), drawing rights of member countries with the IMF and credit arrangements (bilateral and multilateral credits).

The adequacy of international liquidity is in theory only an issue as long as the total amount of assets serving as reserves is limited. This was indeed the inherent problem of the gold standard as well as the Bretton Woods (par-value) regime. Yet after these flaws were overcome and the gold standard abandoned some argued that the issue of providing adequate international liquidity has not been resolved but has effectively disappeared.[28] Accordingly, today those scholars see the issue confined to one remaining question: What is the optimum level of reserves countries should maintain?[29] But whereas it is true that today's international monetary system provides reserve assets which theoretically are available or can be produced in unlimited supply (with the exception of gold), the assumption that the issue has

[25]IMF (2012, p. 10).

[26]Clark and Polak (2002, p. 6).

[27]IMF (2008, p. 97).

[28]Clark and Polak (2002, p. 6 ss).

[29]Clark and Polak (2002, p. 6).

disappeared completely was premature. The fact that assets aren't scarce by nature does not mean they will be made available in sufficient supply when needed. 'Reserve currencies', for example, are first and foremost national currencies governed by national authorities who are primarily pursuing national interests. On the contrary, balance of payment difficulties (occurring when a nation is unable to pay for essential imports or service its debt repayments) can rapidly become acute when foreign loans become inaccessible, due to for example mounting concerns about the sustainability of public debt, and reserves are being drained in an attempt to cope with the import and export fluctuations. Such imbalances have internal and external causes ranging from inappropriate fiscal and monetary policies (e.g. current account and fiscal deficits, high levels of debt) to shocks caused by among others natural disasters or large swings in commodity prices and they can even affect economically sound countries. In addition, the financial crisis of 2007/2008 and the ensuing sovereign debt crisis[30] illustrated once more that solvency concerns can generate an illiquidity crisis which in turn can lead to a solvency problem—a self-fulfilling prophecy in some regards, which cannot be met exclusively by holding an optimum level of reserves according to pre-crisis considerations.

In conclusion, international liquidity does continue to be an underlying issue of international monetary relations but has transformed since it was first discovered by economists from being a mainly theoretical problem with practical consequences into a practical/systemic one driven by market forces as well as financial and political authorities. Nonetheless it remains highly topical.

3.6 The Trilemma of Monetary Policy

Finally, to conclude this chapter on fundamental issues of monetary relations the trilemma of monetary policy will be discussed.[31] The trilemma represents an economic hypothesis based on a finding from empirical studies, which cannot be disregarded without suffering consequences and thus effectively constrains monetary policy choices. The lesson of the trilemma itself is fairly simple: There are three typically desirable, yet jointly unattainable, objectives in monetary policy. Ideally, monetary policy would aim to (1) stabilize exchange-rates (fixed exchange-rates being most stable) and to (2) enable free capital movement while (3) maintaining monetary policy independence (oriented towards domestic goals). Unfortunately, however, there exists a stark tradeoff between these three objectives and only two of them are mutually attainable at any one time.[32] In the past, countries have disregarded this 'rule' and tried to achieve the trinity—failing repeatedly. Although strong empirical evidence and experiences in the past support the argument of the

[30]On how the financial crisis developed into a fiscal crisis see Lastra (2015, p. 309 ss).

[31]The idea was first developed by Fleming (1962, pp. 369–379) and Mundell (1962, pp. 475–485).

[32]Obstfeld et al. (2005, p. 423).

trilemma,[33] the hypothesis is not undisputed and recently *Hélène Rey* argued that the trilemma is in fact only a dilemma, because regardless of the exchange-rate regime national monetary policy would always be constrained by the global financial cycle as long as capital is freely movable.[34] In this context, a read of the IMF's institutional view on capital controls may be of interest as well.[35]

References

Clark P, Polak J (2002) International liquidity and the role of the SDR in the International Monetary System. IMF working paper https://www.imf.org/external/pubs/ft/wp/2002/wp02217.pdf

Cross S (1994) Thoughts on the international monetary system and the future of the IMF. In: Bretton Woods Commission (ed) Bretton Woods: looking to the future, Bretton Woods Commission, Washington D.C, pp C-31–C-38

Fleming M (1962) Domestic financial policies under fixed and floating exchange-rates. IMF Staff Pap 9(3):369–380

Galbis V (1996) Currency convertibility and the fund: review and prognosis. IMF working paper No. 96/39:1–64

Gold J (1976) A report on certain legal developments in the International Monetary Fund. World Association of Lawyers, Washington

Goldberg L (2010) Is the international role of the Dollar changing? Federal Reserve Bank of New York. Curr Issues Econ Finance 16(1). http://www.newyorkfed.org/research/current_issues/ci16-1.pdf

Herrmann C (2007) Play money? Contemporary perspectives on monetary sovereignty. EUI working paper RSCAS 2007/28

IMF (2008) Balance of payment manual, 6th edn. https://www.imf.org/external/np/sta/bop/BOPman.pdf

IMF (2012) Liberalizing capital flows and managing outflows. http://www.imf.org/external/np/pp/eng/2012/031312.pdf

IMF (2014) Annual report on exchange arrangements and exchange restriction. https://www.imf.org/external/pubs/nft/2014/areaers/ar2014.pdf

Kenen P (1983) The role of the dollar as an international currency. Group of Thirty occasional paper No. 13, 1983. Group of Thirty, New York

Lastra R (2015) International financial and monetary law, 2nd edn. Oxford University Press, Oxford

Lerch M (2015) Bitcoin als evolution des geldes (Bitcoins as evolution of money). ZBB/JBB 2015:190–205

Mundell R (1962) Capital mobility and stabilization policy under fixed and flexible exchange-rates. Can J Econ Polit Sci 29(4):475–485

Obstfeld M, Shambaugh J, Taylor A (2005) The Trilemma in history: tradeoffs among Exchange rates, monetary policies and capital mobility. Rev Econ Stat 87(3):423–438

[33]Obstfeld et al. (2005, p. 435 s).

[34]Rey (2015). See also: http://www.economist.com/news/finance-and-economics/21584351-how-can-emerging-economies-protect-themselves-rich-worlds-monetary.

[35]IMF (2012) http://www.imf.org/external/np/pp/eng/2012/111412.pdf.

Polak J (1992) Reserve currency. In: Eatwell J, Milgate M, Newman P (eds) The New Palgrave dictionary of money and finance, vol 3, 1st edn. Palgrave Macmillan UK, Basingstoke, pp 339–342
Proctor C (2012) Mann on the legal aspect of money, 7th edn. Oxford University Press, Oxford
Rey H (2015) Dilemma not Trilemma: the global financial cycle and monetary policy independence, NBER working paper 2015 www.nber.org/papers/w21162

Chapter 4
The International Monetary Constitution: The IMF Articles of Agreement—Institutional Design and Decision-Making

The legal framework of the IMF (or "Fund") is the main source of International Monetary Law besides, of course, general principles derived from customary international law. With a member base of 189 states, the IMF Articles of Agreement enjoy a nearly global binding force and have shaped the international monetary system since its entry into force on 27 December 1945. The agreement is the constitutional treaty of the IMF and has been amended seven times throughout its history.[1]

The words of Sir Joseph Gold, former Legal Counsel of the Fund seem to be a fitting preface for the following chapters:

> The law of the IMF must be analysed in the context of its Articles of Agreement, its By-Laws, Rules and Regulations and the decisions, interpretations, and resolutions of the Executive Board and the Board of Governors of the International Monetary Fund.[2]

4.1 Institutional Design

4.1.1 The IMF within the International Setting

The IMF is an international organisation[3] equipped with legal personality (Art. IX sec. 2 IMF Articles of Agreement) and as such is a subject of international law with the capacity of possessing legal rights and obligations independent of its member states.[4] The seat of the IMF is in Washington D.C, USA, but the IMF maintains

[1]For a list of the first six amendments see Lastra (2015, p. 430 s); for information on the most recent one see http://www.imf.org/external/np/sec/misc/consents.htm.
[2]Printed in: Lastra (2015, p. 430).
[3]For a possible definition of international organizations see Art. 2 (a) of the ILC's Draft Articles on the Responsibility of International Organizations, http://legal.un.org/ilc/texts/instruments/english/draft_articles/9_11_2011.pdf.
[4]On the status of international organizations in international law see Crawford (2012, p. 115 ss and p. 166 ss), ICJ (1949, p. 174 ss).

C. Herrmann and C. Dornacher, *International and European Monetary Law*, SpringerBriefs in Law, DOI 10.1007/978-3-319-57642-8_4

departments and resident representative offices in various other member states.[5] Pursuant to Art. IX sec. 2 IMF Articles of Agreement, the IMF may also enter into international agreements with member states (e.g. for the opening of new resident representative offices) as well as with non-member states (e.g. the 1991 Special Association Agreement between the U.S.S.R and the IMF) and other international organisations (see also Art. X IMF Articles of Agreement). The latter option is of particular significance for conducting the tasks of the IMF. While international organisations are often confined to specific and distinct mandates, their work may nevertheless overlap or impact each other, requiring coordination and complementary work strategies in order to succeed in achieving the desired objectives.[6] Obvious examples of such undertakings are the relations the IMF established with the World Bank[7] and the World Trade Organisation[8] (see the 1996 Agreement between the IMF and the WTO) due to the close links of economic, financial and monetary issues. In this context, the IMF's status as specialized agency of the United Nations (UN) following the 1947 Agreement is also noteworthy.[9] The IMF remains, however, an independent organisation and is, for example, not directly bound by Security Council decisions under Art. 41 and 42 of the UN Charter.[10]

4.1.2 *The Legal Framework of the IMF*

The centrepiece of the legal framework governing the institutional life and work of the IMF are the IMF Articles of Agreement. The role and rank of the agreement is comparable to that of a constitution within a nation state and it is sometimes also formally referred to as the "charter" of the IMF.

In addition, there is a considerable body of administrative law, which has been developed by the institutions of the IMF, substantiating or affecting the performance of imposed obligations and conferred rights under the charter. The administrative law of the IMF consists of by-laws and resolutions adopted by the Board of Governors, rules and regulations by the Executive Board and general administrative orders by the Managing Director.

The vast majority of institutional acts, however, are not abstract legal rules but individual decisions in concrete cases, e.g. assessing the members' compliance with

---

[5]For a list see here: https://www.imf.org/external/country/ResRep/index.aspx.

[6]For an overview of the IMF collaboration with other organisations see https://www.imf.org/external/about/collab.htm.

[7]For a comprehensive summary of the collaboration see: https://www.imf.org/external/np/exr/facts/imfwb.htm.

[8]For a comprehensive summary of the collaboration see: https://www.imf.org/external/np/exr/facts/imfwto.htm.

[9]For a list of all specialized UN agencies see http://www.un.org/Overview/uninbrief/institutions.shtml.

[10]Gianviti (1999, p. 32).

their obligations under the Articles of Agreement. Interestingly, the IMF's legal framework does not provide for a judicial review procedure of IMF decisions. In fact, the IMF is not subject to the jurisdiction of any member state's court or the International Court of Justice (ICJ) for matters arising under the IMF charter (disputes under the special agency agreement with the UN may be referred to the ICJ) unless it agrees to waive its immunity, which in practice the IMF does not do (except for occasional arbitration clauses in certain contracts) (Art. IX sec. 3 IMF Articles of Agreement). A slight deviation from this practice was the establishment of the IMF Administrative Tribunal (Tribunal) in 1994, which serves as an independent judicial forum and is restricted to the resolution of employment disputes arising between the IMF and its staff. Though it is technically not a judicial review tool, since the decisions are only declaratory and not intended to rescind illegal acts, the option to request an authoritative interpretation does exist in the charter: Art. XXIX Articles of Agreement. In case of inter-member or member state/IMF disagreements on the formal interpretation of any provision of the Articles of Agreement, the question may be referred to the Executive Board (with possible appeal to the Board of Governors) which will then issue an authoritative interpretation. Such cases are very rare though and most interpretative work is still done impliedly, albeit non-authoritatively, by day-to-day operational decisions, giving meaning to and implementing the charter and the secondary law.[11]

This lack of judicial control certainly allows the IMF to act promptly and effectively in fulfilling its mandate. Moreover, this focus on self-control, in contrast to a system of checks and balances, was most likely informed by the idea that a technical institution on the international level dealing with monetary issues and equipped with special expertise does not require or is not even capable of being subject to conventional judicial review.[12] Considering the IMF's prominent role in crisis management and the far-reaching effects of its involvement and lending activities, however, the self-control approach may turn out to be inadequate in coping with allegations of improprieties or suspicions of contempt of the rule of law in the long run.

4.1.3 Institutional Design

The IMF is an independent international institution, possessing legal personality, yet its institutional setup and decision-making procedures were designed to reflect its member base structure and composition, specifically taking into account their relative position in the global economy. Therefore, it does not possess a political structure like the UN (one country-one vote principle) but resembles much more

[11]Gianviti (1999, p. 34 ss).

[12]Gianviti (1999, p. 36).

that of a company with its shareholders' meetings, board of directors and chairman of the board.[13]

The formal issue of membership is dealt with in Art. II of the Articles of Agreement and in section 2 it is stipulated that membership 'shall be open to other countries', i.e. other than the original signatories (Art. II sec. 1). The wording ("countries") clearly restricts eligibility or membership to nation states and thus excludes other entities from direct representation within the IMF (see Chap. 6 for the case of the EMU).[14] The formal control of external relations normally suffices to be considered a State by the IMF and members are accepted irrespective of their political system or human rights record (nor is either one a prerequisite to keep the member status).[15] This practice is fully in line with the mandate and purpose of the IMF. Withdrawal from membership is nevertheless possible on both voluntary (Art. XXVI sec. 1 IMF Articles of Agreement) and compulsory (Art. XXVI sec. 2 IMF Articles of Agreement) basis.[16]

As previously stated the IMF is not structured according to the principle "one member one vote". Instead, members are assigned quotas,[17] based broadly on their relative position in the world economy.[18] The individual quota of each member determines how much it contributes to the IMF (subscription of financial resources), how many votes it has (voting power)[19] and how much it can borrow (access to IMF financing). The quotas are denominated in SDRs (Special Drawing Rights), the IMF unit of account. Until recently, the total amount of SDRs was 238.5 billion (329.83 billion US Dollars).[20] However, the 2010 Quota and Governance Reform finally entered into force on January 26, 2016, doubling the total amount of SDRs and significantly realigning quota shares in favour of emerging market countries. The purpose of the reform is to augment the IMF core resources and to facilitate a better reflection of the growing role of dynamic emerging and developing countries in the world economy.[21] The main beneficiaries of this reform are China, Russia, Brazil and India, who will gain influence due to an increased voting power. Despite this shift, the US and the Euro area states will retain voting shares equivalent to

[13]Gianviti (1999, p. 39), Lastra (2015, p. 434).

[14]The only exceptions to this rule are the Special Administrative Regions of China: Hong Kong and Macao, http://www.imf.org/external/country/index.htm#H.

[15]Lastra (2015, p. 434).

[16]Examples for voluntary withdrawal: Poland 1950, Cuba 1964, Indonesia 1965. For compulsory withdrawal: Czechoslovakia 1954.

[17]See https://www.imf.org/external/np/exr/facts/quotas.htm.

[18]For a detailed account see Lastra (2015, p. 437 ss).

[19]Each member has 250 basic votes plus one additional vote for each part of its quota equivalent to 100,000 SDR, Art. XII sec. 5 a Articles of Agreement; Gianviti (1999, p. 38).

[20]IMF Quotas Factsheet, https://www.imf.org/external/np/exr/facts/quotas.htm.

[21]IMF Press Release No. 15/573, 18.12.2015, https://www.imf.org/external/np/sec/pr/2015/pr15573.htm.

16.5% and above respectively, which practically amounts to a veto right for all decisions requiring an 85% majority of the total voting power.[22]

The IMF governance and organisation is structured in a hierarchical fashion and represents its members on various levels, which ensures the accountability of the IMF to the member states' governments.[23] The decision-making organs are listed in Art. XII sec. 1 IMF Articles of Agreement. These are, from top to bottom: The Board of Governors, the Executive Board and the Managing Director.

The Board of Governors—the highest decision-making organ of the IMF—consists of one Governor and one alternate Governor appointed by each member state (Art. XII sec. 2 a IMF Articles of Agreement). The Governors appointed to the Board are usually Finance Ministers or Central Bank Presidents.[24] Notwithstanding their appointment and close link to their respective member state, which is further strengthened by the fact that their service is not remunerated by the IMF, they are entitled to cast the votes allotted to their home country independently and not just on behalf of the respective member state (Art. XII sec. 2 e and h IMF Articles of Agreement).[25]

Meetings are normally held once a year (IMF-World Bank Annual Meeting) and resolutions can be adopted during those meetings or by mail.[26] The (theoretically) preeminent role of the Board of Governors largely stems from the wide range of powers vested in it by Art. XII sec. 2 a IMF Articles of Agreement: "*All powers under this Agreement not conferred directly on the Board of Governors, the Executive Board, or the Managing Director shall be vested in the Board of Governors*". In practice, however, the Board of Governors has delegated its powers in the broadest way possible, namely all those not directly attributed to itself, to the Executive Board (Art. XII sec. 2 b IMF Articles of Agreement). Thus, all powers which are not conferred upon a specific organ, must be read as powers exercised by the Executive Board. The consequence of this delegation is a massive shift in decision making activity from the Board of Governors to the Executive Board. Notwithstanding the delegation, the general understanding is though that the Board of Governors is not divested of its powers and may still act or intervene. Additionally, the Executive Board may only exercise the delegated powers in accordance with decisions taken by the (superior) Board of Governors (this refers mostly to by-laws and resolutions) and is not allowed to further sub-delegate the delegated powers.[27]

---

[22]For a detailed study of the shift in quota shares see https://www.imf.org/external/np/sec/pr/2011/pdfs/quota_tbl.pdf.

[23]IMF at a Glance Factsheet, http://www.imf.org/external/np/exr/facts/glance.htm.

[24]Gianviti (1999, p. 39).

[25]Gianviti (1999, p. 45 ss).

[26]Gianviti (1999, p. 39).

[27]Lastra (2015, p. 435); for a detailed account of the interpretative issues concerning the delegation of powers see Gianviti (1999, p. 40 ss).

Consequently, the everyday business of the IMF is carried out in the Washington D.C. headquarters by the Executive Board (Art. XII sec. 3 IMF Articles of Agreement), which is supported by the professional staff of the IMF.[28] Depending on the workload, the Executive Board usually meets in full day sessions at least three times a week. Originally, the twenty-four Executive Directors forming the Executive Board were partly appointed (the US, Japan, Germany, France and the UK named their own Directors) and partly elected by single or groups of countries, known as 'constituencies'. Following the entry into force of the 2010 Quota and Governance Reform, this distinction was abandoned in favour of an all-elected body of Directors. Although the size of the Executive Board remains the same, there are two fewer Directors from advanced European countries. Similarly to the Governors, the status of Directors is not that of a formal representative of their constituents. Conversely, the Directors have a fiduciary duty to the IMF to fulfil their obligations pursuing the objectives listed in Art. I IMF Articles of Agreement and are in breach of that duty should they base their decisions exclusively on instructions issued by their home countries.[29]

Finally, the Managing Director is selected for a renewable term of five years by the Executive Board and serves as Chairman of the latter as well as the Head of Staff of the IMF (Art. XII sec. 4 IMF Articles of Agreement).[30] Under the 1947 Special Agency Agreement with the UN, he or she also serves as "executive head" of the IMF. Four Deputy Managing Directors (Office of the Managing Director), who are appointed by the Managing Director with the approval of the Executive Board, assist the Managing Director in the discharge of his/her duties. In his/her function as chairman, he/she does not have a vote except to break a deadlock in case of an equal division of votes.[31]

Aside of these main decision-making organs, there are several groups and committees which shape the work of the IMF through advice and guidance. Note that none of them possess any decision-making power.[32] Nevertheless, they play an important role within the governance structure of the IMF.[33] With regard to the organisational chart of the IMF a mention must be made of the International Monetary and Financial Committee (IMFC) and the Joint IMF-World Bank Development Committee, who were both established as advisory committees by the Board of Governors pursuant to Art. XII sec. 2 j IMF Articles of Agreement. They roughly mirror the size and composition of the Board of Executives with

[28]Lastra (2015, p. 435).

[29]Gianviti (1999, p. 45 ss), Lastra (2015, p. 435).

[30]IMF Decision Making Factsheet, https://www.imf.org/external/np/exr/facts/govern.htm.

[31]Gianviti (1999, p. 48).

[32]IMF, A Guide To Committees, Groups, And Clubs Factsheet, http://www.imf.org/external/np/exr/facts/groups.htm.

[33]A comprehensive guide to all committees, groups and clubs can be found here: http://www.imf.org/external/np/exr/facts/groups.htm.

twenty-four and twenty-five members respectively. Today, both committees represent a key source for the provision of strategic direction to the work and policies of the IMF.[34]

4.2 Decision-Making Procedures/Processes

The validity of an administrative decision generally depends on three conditions: The competent organ acted, the required procedure was observed and the content is in accordance with substantive requirements.

The competence of the acting organ is rarely an issue due to the rather clear-cut division of powers between the Board of Governors and the Executive Board (see above). A slightly more complicated issue is the distinction between powers of the Executive Board and the Managing Director, because the majority of the Managing Director's powers are exercised under the 'direction' or 'general control' of the Executive Board (Art. XII sec. 4 b IMF Articles of Agreement). Meanwhile, the precise identification of the respective competences is, however, facilitated by a constantly evolving body of decisions and practices e.g. see N-16 Staff Regulations.[35]

In terms of procedural requirements, the rules differ depending on the organ in question and the subject matter at hand. Both collegiate organs—the Board of Governors and the Executive Board—are only capable of making decisions if a certain quorum is met (Board of Governors see Art. XII sec. 2 d; Executive Board see Art. XII sec. 3 h). Furthermore, the Executive Board usually does not decide based on a formal vote (except when specifically requested by a Director) but on consensus, which is determined by the Managing Director, who ascertains the sense of the meeting (C-10 The Executive Board Rule[36]). Presumably uncontroversial decisions, which do not require prior discussion, may also be approved on a lapse of time basis. In this case the Managing Director will circulate a proposed decision, which is deemed to be approved after the expiration of a specified period if no formal meeting was requested by a Director (a rare case of silence constituting acceptance).[37] The general rule is that a simple majority of the votes cast suffices for the successful adoption of a decision (Art. XII sec. 5 c IMF Articles of Agreement). In addition, there are two types of special majority: A majority of votes cast representing either 70 or 85% of the total voting power. The flip side of special majorities is effectively a veto right for members/a minority possessing or

[34]IMF, A Guide To Committees, Groups, And Clubs Factsheet, http://www.imf.org/external/np/exr/facts/groups.htm.

[35]Gianviti (1999, p. 50); for N-16 Staff Regulations see: https://www.imf.org/external/pubs/ft/bl/rr14.htm.

[36]See https://www.imf.org/external/pubs/ft/bl/rr03.htm.

[37]See for more detail Gianviti (1999, p. 51).

accumulating 15–30% of the total voting power (e.g. the US and the Euro area states or the EU Member States). The special majority requirement remains an exception though and is reserved for significant decisions like the adjustment of quotas (Art. III sec. 2 c IMF Articles of Agreement). A single provision in a proposed decision may already trigger the special majority requirement for the adoption of the whole document. If an adopted decision is subsequently amended, the majority requirement will depend on the content of the amendment as well as on the section which is to be amended. It does not matter, however, whether the decision as a whole was originally adopted by a special majority.[38]

Lastly, there are substantive requirements for the adoption of decisions. Of course, there exists a large amount of substantive rules governing the administrative output of the IMF organs; an exhaustive list would probably create more confusion than understanding. Therefore, this Chapter will merely focus on the general principles, which must be observed across all decision-making processes. Overall, (1) all decisions must be consistent with the Charter; (2) all decisions must be in accordance with higher norms (decisions of a superior organ); and (3) all individual decisions must be consistent with all regulations made by that organ.[39]

In particular, this means that the IMF can only adopt decisions which are within the realm of the purposes outlined in Art. I IMF Articles of Agreement. The purposes are defined in rather broad terms, allowing room for interpretation and a large degree of latitude in the formulation of policies. In the past, the IMF has used this discretion in order to adapt to changing circumstances and needs. The uniform treatment of members and the rule of non-retroactivity represent far more tangible principles in this regard. Both are not explicitly mentioned in the charter but implied in certain provisions and regarded as general principles of IMF law. The uniform treatment rule is derived from Art. V sec. 3 b IMF Articles of Agreement and applies to all decisions with one exception: Art. V sec. 12 f ii) IMF Articles of Agreement enables the IMF to specially assist its poorest members in their balance of payment problems ("*(…) to developing members in difficult circumstances, and for this purpose the Fund shall* ***take into account the level of per capita income***"). The principle of non-retroactivity on the other hand renders all retroactive decisions to the detriment of IMF members or staff illegal. The principle is not as absolute as this brief definition may imply. For example, the rule does not apply to ongoing processes. An increase in the rate of interest on outstanding loans can indeed be valid for charges and interests accruing after the decision became effective, notwithstanding the fact that the original reason for the accruing of the charges/interests (the loan agreement and the discharge of the loan) predates the decision. In summary, it is necessary to differentiate between retroactivity and immediate effect of a decision.[40]

[38]Gianviti (1999, p. 52).

[39]Gianviti (1999, p. 54).

[40]Gianviti (1999, p. 59 s).

With regard to (2) and (3), the general principle involved is the hierarchy of norms, to which all organs—specifically the Executive Board and the Managing Director—must adhere. The rule itself is pretty straightforward. Disputes usually only arise due to differing interpretations of the norms.

If all these conditions (and all additional specific requirements applicable in the concrete case) are met, the decision will be valid and binding.

References

Crawford J (2012) Brownlies Principles of Public International Law, 8th edn. Oxford University Press, Oxford

Gianviti F (1999) Decision making in the IMF. In: Current developments in monetary and financial law, vol 1, IMF, Washington, pp 31–67

ICJ (1949) Reparations for injuries suffered in the service of the UN, ICJ Reports 1949. http://www.icj-cij.org/docket/files/4/1835.pdf

Lastra R (2015) International Financial and monetary law, 2nd edn. Oxford University Press, Oxford

Chapter 5
The International Monetary Constitution: The IMF Articles of Agreement—Substantive Legal Obligations

While the IMF's mandate is to ensure the stability of the international monetary system through surveillance, technical and financial assistance, membership in the IMF comes not only with benefits but also with obligations. Its objectives (Art. I IMF Articles of Agreement) can only be achieved, if all members fulfill certain requirements and comply with a certain standard, enabling the envisaged system to function. To this end, the Articles of Agreement impose a set of substantive legal obligations of a varying legal nature upon the member states. The main duties are comprised in Art. VIII (convertibility) and Art. IV (exchange arrangements) IMF Articles of Agreement. Compliance with these obligations is closely monitored and enforced by the IMF.[1] A breach of any of these duties may result in sanctions (see Art. XXVI sec. 2 IMF Articles of Agreement) with three escalating levels depending on the duration and severity of the violation: (1) ineligibility to use the general IMF resources, (2) temporary suspension of voting rights and (3) compulsory withdrawal from the IMF (rarely applied in practice).

Proctor advocates a broader interpretation of the charter, arguing that the duties comprised in the IMF Articles of Agreement are not only owed to the IMF (the sole explicit holder of sanctioning power under the charter) but also impliedly to all other member states.[2] Consequently, this would entitle member states to enforce their mutual duties separately or in addition to the IMF sanctions in the event of a violation, e.g. take proportionate countermeasures. Notwithstanding the mutuality of rights and obligations entailed by being a member of an international organization, the argument is flawed. The bilateral or multilateral attempt of a proportionate response by suspending obligations, e.g. convertibility, toward a member in default may jeopardize the entire purpose of the IMF and lead back to a system of external monetary policies driven by national interests. Therefore, the favorable interpretation is that the power to sanction and enforce any obligation arising under the IMF Articles of Agreement is only vested in the IMF itself.

[1]Lastra (2015, p. 450).
[2]Proctor (2012, p. 589 s).

C. Herrmann and C. Dornacher, *International and European Monetary Law*,
SpringerBriefs in Law, DOI 10.1007/978-3-319-57642-8_5

5.1 Convertibility

As explained in Chap. 3, convertibility broadly means the ability to exchange domestic currency for foreign currency and to use foreign currency for transactions.[3] Yet, the jurisdiction of the IMF is limited to current account convertibility due to largely historical reasons and in particular *White*[4] and *Keynes*[5]—the intellectual fathers of the Bretton Woods system—favoring control of capital movements. This limitation remains controversial but has not yet led to an amendment of the charter (for more detail see below).[6]

The core obligation is set out in Art. VIII sec. 2 IMF Articles of Agreement, commonly referred to as the duty to maintain current account convertibility. The provision is divided into two parts with different legal natures: section 2 a) contains a public international law rule directed at member states and section 2 b) stipulates a rule of private international law/conflict of laws[7] aimed at hindering a circumvention of section 2 a) by the contractual practice of private citizens.[8] For the purpose of this book the focus will lie on the public international law obligation.

The scope of Art. VIII sec. 2 a) IMF Articles of Agreement: It does not automatically apply to all members upon joining the IMF. Conversely, members can opt (see Art. XIV sec. 1) to avail themselves of the transitional status prescribed in Art. XIV sec. 2 IMF Articles of Agreement by notification to the IMF. These transitional arrangements allow the member to maintain and adapt restrictions which were already in place prior to their IMF membership. Likewise, the transitional period formally only ends once the member state is prepared to accept the duties comprised in Art. VIII sec. 2, 3, 4 IMF Articles of Agreement. The IMF does, however, review the progress of the transition annually and members are obliged not to extend that period unduly.[9] Currently 168 of the 189 member states fall within the scope of Art. VIII IMF Articles of Agreement.[10]

Substantively, the duty to maintain current account convertibility prohibits any restrictions on the making of payments and transfers for current international transactions which were not previously notified to and approved of by the IMF.[11] The term ‘payments for current transactions’ is defined in Art. XXX d IMF Articles of Agreement and encompasses more transactions than the traditional definition used by economists, e.g. the inclusion of some transfers from capital movements,

---

[3]Galbis (1996, p. 3).

[4]See White’s proposal, reproduced in Horsefield (1986, pp. 47 and 63).

[5]See Keynes’ proposal, reproduced in Horsefield (1986, p. 13).

[6]Lastra (2015, pp. 450 s).

[7]Lastra (2015, p. 452), Proctor (2012, p. 410 s).

[8]For a detailed analysis of Art. VIII sec. 2 b IMF Articles of Agreement see Proctor (2012, pp. 410–437).

[9]Lastra (2015, p. 452).

[10]IMF (2014, p. 31).

[11]See also Proctor (2012, pp. 612–617), who presents a comprehensive overview of the obligation.

such as amortization of loans. Generally, though, the obligation is limited to current account convertibility, thus member states remain free to restrict or control capital movements; they are in fact explicitly allowed to do so (see Art. VI sec. 3 IMF Articles of Agreement). The latter provision affects the assertion of the scope of the IMF competences and precludes any attempts to broaden the IMF's jurisdiction with respect to capital movement by means of extensive interpretation forgoing a formal amendment procedure.[12] Concerning the approval of restrictions, the IMF has developed a large body of policies over the years which are intended to direct the individual decision. Balance of payments difficulties[13] as well as national or international security considerations are, for example, generally considered legitimate reasons to introduce temporary restrictions.[14] The decision of approval (or disapproval) may be communicated explicitly or impliedly on a lapse-of-time basis.[15]

Temporarily exempt from the obligation are member states whose currency has been declared scarce pursuant to Art. VII sec. 3 b). The declaration serves as a general authorization of the member state to implement restrictions it deems necessary to limit the demand for the scarce currency without the IMF's prior approval. The exemption expires once the declaration is withdrawn by the IMF.

Even though the free movement of capital is not a duty associated with IMF membership, most developed countries have nevertheless liberalized their capital markets. Moreover, despite the fact that capital flows expose countries to sometimes great volatility, private capital flows continue to constitute a main source of financing for developed as well as developing countries and the overall trend towards liberalization remains unbroken despite the global financial crisis of 2007.[16] Yet, so far the member states were not able to muster enough political willpower or momentum to transform the global trend into hard law.[17] At present, there is only the IMF's attempt to provide consistent policy advice for its members on the subject matter.[18] In summary, three categories of IMF members can be distinguished: members that (1) still operate with restrictions; (2) maintain current account convertibility (Art. VIII); (3) maintain full convertibility (no obligation).[19]

---

[12] Lastra (2015, p. 453).

[13] Executive Board, Decision No. 1034-(60/27), 06/01/1960, para. 2. Similar exemptions are foreseen in the WTO law under Art. XV:9, XII, XIII GATT and Art. XII:1 GATS; for more information in this regard see Viterbo (2012, p. 205 ss).

[14] See IMF, Decision No. 144-(52/51), 08/14/1952. For a detailed analysis of allowed exchange restrictions see Viterbo (2012, p. 169 ss).

[15] Lastra (2015, p. 451).

[16] Lastra (2015, p. 454).

[17] Lastra (2015, p. 454 s).

[18] IMF (2012) http://www.imf.org/external/np/pp/eng/2012/111412.pdf; Viterbo provides a detailed study of capital controls under the IMF Articles of Agreement in: Viterbo (2012), pp. 178 ss.

[19] Lastra (2015, p. 453).

5.2 Exchange-Rate Regimes

The IMF Articles of Agreement's exchange-rate provisions used to be virtually self-enforcing, universally imposing the par-value system, representing 'hard' legal obligations. In the aftermath of the gold standard's demise and the ensuing breakdown of the par-value system, the provision was significantly altered by the Second Amendment and lost considerably in terms of decisiveness. Art. IV sec. 2 b IMF Articles of Agreement now gives members a free choice in determining their exchange-rate arrangement. The various options when designing such an exchange-rate regime as well as the current practice of member states were already outlined in Chap. 3.[20] In a nutshell, the diversity of exchange-rate regimes could hardly be any greater and the probability of a (re-)introduction of the par-value system (possible under Art. IV sec. 4 IMF Articles of Agreement) any more remote. Moreover, despite the IMF's purpose "*to promote exchange stability, to maintain orderly exchange arrangements among members, and to avoid competitive exchange depreciation*" (Art. I (iii) IMF Articles of Agreement), the charter presently lacks a clearly defined, enforceable legal duty to maintain stable currencies.[21] This assessment is further underpinned by the rather vague—practically uncontrollable—formulations of the other obligations listed in Art. IV IMF Articles of Agreement ("endeavor…"; "seek to promote…").[22]

An exception in this context is the ban on "exchange-rate manipulation" (Art. IV sec. 1 (iii) IMF Articles of Agreement). The wording of this section clearly prohibits a specific external relations strategy/conduct, namely to manipulate "*exchange-rates or the international monetary system in order to prevent effective balance of payments adjustments or to gain an unfair competitive advantage over other members*". But again the clarity ends there. The only firm conclusion Art. IV sec. 1 (iii) allows to draw is that a policy can only be deemed illegal if it fulfills an objective element ("manipulation") and a subjective element ("in order to").[23] In the absence of a definition by the IMF charter itself, it remains unclear whether 'manipulation' requires an active behavior by a member state or even whether a movement of the exchange-rate is necessary or whether a prevention of movement would suffice too.[24] Further difficulties for the interpretation and application of the norm arise in connection with other obligations and prerogatives of member states like Art. IV sec. 1 (ii), asking states to promote monetary stability while simultaneously leaving them a free choice of exchange-rate regimes. From the regulatory

[20]See IMF (2014, p. 31).

[21]Proctor (2012, p. 593).

[22]Lastra (2015, p. 423 s).

[23]Herrmann (2010, p. 41); see also Executive Board, Decision No. 12/89, 07/18/2012, Annex para. 2, https://www.imf.org/external/np/sec/pn/2012/pn1289.htm.

[24]Gold (1989, p. 109), Herrmann (2010, p. 41).

interplay of both, one can derive that an intervention in foreign exchange markets does not per se constitute an illegal practice, since a currency peg—legal under IMF law—cannot be upheld without interventions by the respective monetary authority.[25] Therefore, what distinguishes a legal and legitimate intervention from an illegal and illegitimate manipulation?

The charter largely leaves the answer to the IMF bodies (in this case the Executive Board), who would have to develop and substantiate the concept of exchange-rate manipulation in practice. Some guidance concerning the interpretation of Art. IV sec. 1 (iii) IMF Articles of Agreement is indeed given in the Annex of the Executive Board Decision on Bilateral and Multilateral Surveillance.[26] The Annex contains instructions for an objective assessment and specifies that only measures "targeted at—and actually affect(ting)—the level of an exchange-rate" (para. 2 (a)) can constitute a manipulation, regardless of the effect being an exchange-rate movement or a prevention thereof.[27] Furthermore it clarifies the meaning of the subjective element, requiring an intent by the alleged manipulator to secure an undervalued exchange-rate in order to increase net exports (para. 2 (b)).

When presented with the opportunity,[28] however, the Executive Board did not make any formal decision or impose any sanctions. Especially with respect to the subjective element an exchange-rate manipulation remains difficult to prove. Meanwhile, some member states are trying to include a more effective prohibition of currency manipulation in international trade agreements, see for example the negotiation process of the TPP,[29] but haven't been successful thus far.[30]

In conclusion, the prohibition contained in the IMF charter remains a toothless tool and the alterations introduced by the Second Amendment resulted in a functional shift for the IMF, placing surveillance front and center on the IMF agenda.[31]

---

[25]Herrmann (2010, p. 41).

[26]Executive Board, Decision No. 12/89, 07/18/2012, https://www.imf.org/external/np/sec/pn/2012/pn1289.htm.

[27]Herrmann noted that this would typically exclude domestic economic and fiscal policies from the scope of Art. IV sec. 1 (iii) IMF Articles of Agreement, since they are usually not targeted at exchange-rates even though they may affect them, Herrmann (2010, p. 44).

[28]The case of Sweden 1982, described in Lastra (2015, p. 424); for an analysis of the alleged manipulation exercised by China see Herrmann (2010).

[29]For the full text of the agreement see: https://ustr.gov/trade-agreements/free-trade-agreements/trans-pacific-partnership/tpp-full-text.

[30]The TTP countries were in the end only able to agree on a joint declaration banning any exchange-rate manipulation, reaffirming the obligation under the IMF charter. Declarations are soft law and thus not binding under international law. They do, however, generate peer pressure.

[31]For the treatment of exchange-rate manipulations under WTO Law—in particular if a manipulation can constitute a breach of Art. XV GATT or represent a prohibited export subsidy—see Herrmann (2010, pp. 46 ss).

5.3 IMF Surveillance

The IMF performs three different kinds of functions: Surveillance, Art. IV IMF Articles of Agreement (regulatory nature); financial assistance Art. V sec. 3 IMF Articles of Agreement (sui generis nature, see next chapter); technical assistance Art. V sec. 2 b IMF Articles of Agreement (advisory nature, see below). Depending on the perspective, all three can either be perceived as instruments to accomplish the mandate (IMF view) or as services provided by the IMF (member view).[32] In contrast to financial and technical assistance, which are voluntary and only provided upon explicit request from a member state, surveillance is mandatory and universally exercised over all members.

Surveillance essentially is the monitoring of the members' compliance with the IMF 'code of conduct' as prescribed and expressed in the Articles of Agreement (mostly obligations of Art. IV). Traditionally, surveillance focused on exchange-rate regimes, exchange-rates and balance of payments. In the wake of financial crises, it was expanded over time to also cover assessments of economic and financial policies with special attention to sectoral, structural and institutional issues.[33] The legal basis for surveillance is embedded in Art. IV sec. 3 a) and b) IMF Articles of Agreement. In addition to this provision, three Executive Board Decisions from 1977,[34] 2007[35] and 2012[36] serve as the regulatory foundation for surveillance, providing a more detailed picture of the task. The Decisions outline the guiding principles and define the subject and modalities of surveillance.

The exercise of surveillance is a complex endeavour, which requires nuanced decisions and farsighted judgements on behalf of the IMF institutions. It illustrates the fundamental transformation of the IMF system from simple enforcement of the par-value regime—a rule-based system—to a system centred around the exercise of discretion.[37] The transformation was aided by the broad scope of purposes facilitating a wide-ranging oversight mechanism, capable to adapt to changing circumstances and needs. Consequently, surveillance as exercised today was reshaped by the experiences with the financial crisis in the late 1990s and most recently to improve the monitoring of financial stability and sectoral policies.[38] It is important to keep in mind though that regardless of new aspects, tools or even insights produced by the extended "surveillance" practice, strictly speaking only the monitoring of the obligations in Art. IV IMF Articles of Agreement constitutes

---

[32] Lastra (2015, p. 455).

[33] Lastra (2015, p. 456).

[34] Executive Board, Decision No. 5392-(77/63) of 29 April 1977 as amended.

[35] Executive Board, Decision of 15 June 2007: Bilateral surveillance of member policies, https://www.imf.org/external/np/sec/pn/2007/pn0769.htm#decision.

[36] Executive Board, An integrated surveillance decision of 17 July 2012, http://www.imf.org/external/np/pp/eng/2012/071712.pdf.

[37] Guitián (1992, p. 8 ss).

[38] Lastra (2015, p. 461).

surveillance and is sanctionable under Art. XXVI IMF Articles of Agreement; everything else falls under the category of technical assistance.[39] Generally, three types of surveillance are distinguishable: (1) bilateral, through the consultation process foreseen in Art. IV IMF Articles of Agreement; (2) multilateral, published twice a year in the 'world economic outlook report' and the 'global financial stability report'; (3) regional, by examining regional developments such as the EU or Euro area.

The code of conduct or more precisely the obligations set out in Art. IV IMF Articles of Agreement, which is/are to be overseen, comprises provisions that are positive (sec. 1 (i), (ii), (iv) = goals) and negative (sec. 1 (iii) = prohibition) in character as well as formulated in soft (sec. 1 (i), (ii)) and hard (sec. 1 (iii), (iv)) terms. The characterisation as soft refers to the fact that the respective section does not impose a legal obligation to achieve a certain objective but only requires the exercise of reasonable effort from the member states.[40] The soft formulation corresponds with the division of competences between the IMF and its members. While sec. 1 (i) and (ii) fall within the scope of domestic policies (core aspect of monetary sovereignty) sec. 1 (iii) and (iv) relate to external policies (main jurisdiction of the IMF).[41] Furthermore, effective surveillance is only possible if member states cooperate and supply all information necessary to perform the task. Therefore, members are obliged to furnish the relevant information to the IMF according to Art. IV sec. 3 b and Art. VIII sec. 5 IMF Articles of Agreement.

In practice, surveillance is mainly conducted through bilateral consultations (a mostly formalised process). The consultation process begins with an IMF staff visit (so called IMF 'mission') to each member state in annual intervals. Such visits mainly serve to gather relevant information and to hold meetings with state officials. The thereby acquired information will then be reviewed and assessed by the IMF staff. Subsequently, this review forms the basis for further consultations with member state authorities, which would normally at this stage address the effectiveness of the implemented policies or prospective changes to improve the effectiveness or correct undesirable developments. After this round of discussions is closed, the IMF mission often forwards a statement containing their preliminary findings to the member state before submitting the final report to the Executive Board. Once it has received the official report, the Executive Board will discuss its content and agree on specific conclusions. Finally, the Executive Board will send a summary of the conclusions drawn to the respective government. The publication of the summary is not compulsory and will only take place with the express consent of the member state.[42] As mentioned above, in addition to the rather formal bilateral

---

[39]Gianviti is critical of this extensive development and warns of the effects of peer pressure which does not specifically correspond with one of the listed obligations, Gianviti (2003, pp. 42 ss).

[40]Proctor (2012, p. 592), Gianviti (2003, p. 46).

[41]Gianviti (2003, pp. 40 ss).

[42]For a detailed outline of the process see Lastra (2015, p. 460).

consultations the surveillance activity of the IMF is informed and supplemented by other inquiries, assessments or joint ventures as well, which for the most part belong to the realm of another function—technical assistance, such as the Financial Sector Assessment Program (FSAP)[43] and the G-20 Mutual Assessment Program (G-20 MAP).[44,45] The FSAP is a joint World Bank–IMF project, which was originally voluntary but now is mandatory for twenty-nine jurisdictions with systemically important financial sectors. The G-20 MAP essentially represents a peer pressure tool.[46] As much as a clear-cut distinction between functions and their exercise would be desirable from a legal perspective, in practice the interplay was always a key feature of the IMF structure and has proven decisive in maintaining a stable international monetary system.

5.4 Technical Assistance

Technical assistance for member states means assistance by offering advice and training (Art. V sec. 2 b IMF Articles of Agreement). Even though the IMF competes in this area with private consultancies it remains in a fairly unique position due to its expertise gained through decades of surveillance and the advantages of receiving technical and financial assistance from a single source. Yet technical assistance is not a members' prerogative. It is generally only granted upon request and sometimes dismissed or discouraged by the IMF due to a shortage in resources or other reasons.[47] Like most other functions of the IMF technical assistance evolved over time from basic support for the creation of central banks and financial ministries in the 1960s to a prominent role in the transition of centrally planned to market economies by the provision of extensive training in banking, monetary and fiscal policy areas in the 1990s. Most recently, the IMF's technical assistance refocused on the strengthening of the international financial architecture, largely due to an increased demand in that regard following the fallout of the global financial crisis. Incidentally, the provision of legal advice by the Funds' Legal Department also falls under '(legal) technical assistance'.[48]

[43]See http://www.imf.org/external/np/exr/facts/fsap.htm.

[44]See http://www.imf.org/external/np/exr/facts/g20map.htm.

[45]For a detailed list of other programs with significance for surveillance see Rendak (2014).

[46]For more details on both programs see Lastra (2015, p. 461 ss).

[47]Lastra (2015, p. 482 s).

[48]Lastra (2015, p. 483). Published reports of assistance provided to member states can be found here: http://www.imf.org/en/Publications/SPROLLs/Technical-assistance-country-reports.

References

Galbis V (1996) Currency convertibility and the fund: review and prognosis. IMF working paper No. 96/39, pp 1–64

Gianviti F (2003) Evolving role and challenges for the IMF. In: Norton J, Andenas M (eds) International monetary and financial law upon entering the new millennium: a tribute to Sir Joseph gold and ruth gold. British Institute of International & Comparative Law, London, pp 29–70

Gold J (1989) Exchange-rates in international law and organizations. American Bar Association, Chicago

Guitián M (1992) The Unique nature of the responsibilities of the IMF. Pamphlet series, No. 46. IMF, Washington. https://www.imf.org/external/pubs/ft/pam/pam46/pam46con.htm

Herrmann C (2010) Don Yuan: China's "selfish" exchange-rate policy and international economic law. In: Herrmann C, Krajewski C, Terhechte J (eds) European yearbook of international economic law 2010, Springer, Heidelberg, pp 31–51

Horsefield J (ed) (1986) The international monetary fund 1945–1965, vol 3: documents. IMF, Washington

IMF (2014) Annual report on exchange arrangements and exchange restriction 2014. https://www.imf.org/external/pubs/nft/2014/areaers/ar2014.pdf

Lastra R (2015) International financial and monetary law, 2nd edn. Oxford University Press, Oxford

Proctor C (2012) Mann on the legal aspects of money, 7th edn. Oxford University Press, Oxford

Rendak N (2014) Monitoring and surveillance at the International Monetary System—what can be learnt from the trade field. In: Cottier et al (eds) The rule of law in monetary affairs. Cambridge University Press, Cambridge pp 204–232

Viterbo A (2012) International economic law and monetary measures, 1st edn. Edward Elgar Publishing, Cheltenham

Chapter 6
IMF Lending (Financial Assistance)

From a member state's perspective, providing financial assistance is probably considered the core responsibility of the IMF and a key advantage of membership. Art. V IMF Articles of Agreement authorises the Fund to perform financial assistance and to develop suitable policies for its lending activities in order to remedy actual or potential balance of payment problems of member states. Yet unlike banks, development organizations or private creditors the IMF does not offer financial support for specific projects nor for balancing out purely fiscal disequilibria. In short, the IMF deals with issues of illiquidity, not of insolvency.[1]

6.1 Financial Architecture and IMF Resources

6.1.1 Financial Architecture

All financial functions of the IMF are administered by the Finance Department, which is an organisational unit of the Fund.[2] The entire operational business is conducted through three different accounting entities (no organizational units), which are themselves further subdivided into special accounts dedicated to specific kinds of transactions or assets and liabilities: The General Department; the SDR Department and the Administered Accounts.[3]

With regard to financial assistance, the most important accounts are the General Department and the Administered Accounts. In particular the General Department with its three sub-accounts—the General Resource Account (GRA); the Special Disbursement Account (SDA) and the Investment Account (IA)—is the main

[1]IMF factsheet, IMF lending, https://www.imf.org/external/np/exr/facts/howlend.htm.
[2]Lastra (2015, p. 440); this chapter draws heavily on Lastra's excellent and much more comprehensive analysis of IMF lending.
[3]For more details see IMF (2001, p. 19 ss), Lastra (2015, p. 440 ss).

C. Herrmann and C. Dornacher, *International and European Monetary Law*, SpringerBriefs in Law, DOI 10.1007/978-3-319-57642-8_6

vehicle for transactions between member states and the IMF. Its balance sheet displays the assets (member's currencies, IMF's own holdings of gold and SDRs) and liabilities of the IMF. While the bulk of the lending activity is processed through the GRA (via "drawings", see below), which is the principal account of the IMF, the SDA is used for the receipt and re-investment of the IMF's gold-sale profits and for inter-IMF-account transfers.[4] The IA on the other hand, the most recent addition to the General Department, was established to generate income through new sources (for the traditional IMF resources see below).[5] The other part of the IMF's lending activities is conducted through Administered Accounts and in form of loans (for the difference to "drawings" see below). An example of Administered Accounts are the various 'trusts'. Conversely, the SDR Department is not used for the provision of financial assistance. It simply shows the assets and liabilities of the other SDR holders (i.e. other than the IMF), which are mostly comprised of member states but can also include non-members, see Art. XVII sec. 3 Articles of Agreement,[6] whereupon SDRs are allocated to SDR Department participants proportionally to their quota (Art. XV sec. 1 IMF Articles of Agreements). Participation in the SDR Department, however, is voluntary.[7] The use of SDRs is further regulated by the 'designation mechanism', Art. XIX sec. 5 IMF Articles of Agreement, under which the IMF can force certain participants to accept SDRs in exchange for freely usable currencies (i.e. US Dollar, Euro, Japanese Yen, Pound Sterling). Similarly to a legal tender rule at national level, this mechanism protects the relevance and function of SDRs by ensuring their convertibility and usability.

6.1.2 Financial Resources

The premise for any provision of financial assistance is the availability of financial means/resources and the Fund is no exception to this rule. There are three main financial sources for the IMF: Subscriptions of members, borrowing and contribution-based trust funds. The sum of all member subscriptions (currently 476.8 billion SDR) forms the capital base of the IMF.[8] The subscription is determined by the assigned quota, an amount calculated by the IMF and expressed in SDR (Art. III sec. 1 IMF Articles of Agreement). It is payable in full to the IMF and consists of up to 25% of reserve assets (SDR or reserve currencies) and the remaining part of the member's currency. The 25% reserve segment is usually referred to as the reserve asset portion and directly corresponds with an instant liquid claim of the member against the Fund ("reserve tranche position"), allowing

[4]Lastra (2015, p. 441).

[5]IMF (2014, p. 107).

[6]See for example Art. 30 sec. 5 ESCB Statute.

[7]Lastra (2015, p. 442).

[8]Lastra (2015, p. 438).

it to exchange its own currency for reserve assets in order to meet balance of payment problems upon demand. Therefore, the reserve tranche position has a dual nature: it simultaneously represents a part of the IMF's resources and a part of the member's international reserve assets. Consequently, the use of the reserve tranche position is not a use of IMF credit.[9] This conclusion is also supported by the definition of reserve tranche purchases (an exchange of currencies is technically always a purchase) in Art. XXX c) IMF Articles of Agreement. Any requests for reserve assets beyond that reserve tranche position—once the member's subscription to the IMF consists entirely of its own currency—are requests for IMF credit.

In order to supplement its capital base and to prevent potential liquidity inadequacies in times of crisis, the IMF began early on to borrow via multilateral and bilateral borrowing arrangements. Of special significance due to sheer volume (up to 370 billion SDR) are the two existing multilateral borrowing arrangements the New Arrangements to Borrow (NAB) and the General Arrangement to Borrow (GAB).[10] Joint lenders in this case are 38 member states, which provide resources independently of their subscriptions, and financial institutions.

Another form of borrowing—as the resources do not stem from the IMF capital base—are trusts. Trusts are funds designated to be used for specific types of loans and supplied by voluntary contributions of member states and the IMF (Art. V sec. 2 b IMF Articles of Agreement). The thereby obtained financial means are dispensed into Administered Accounts for which the IMF acts as a trustee.[11]

6.2 Types of IMF Facilities

During the work and life of the Fund's institutions a proliferation of facilities and corresponding policies occurred that makes it difficult to see through the unduly complex structure of the IMF lending activity. A general distinction can be drawn though between concessional (Art. V sec. 2 b IMF Articles of Agreement) and non-concessional (Art. V sec. 3 a IMF Articles of Agreement) facilities.[12] The distinction is not only one of modalities but also of different techniques to provide the required financial assistance. Non-concessional financing is typically available in form of purchase and repurchase arrangements of reserve assets and is also referred to as drawing on the general resources of the IMF.[13] Whereas concessional financing is conducted via loans and the resources usually stem from the trust

[9]IMF (2001, p. 66).

[10]See https://www.imf.org/external/np/exr/facts/gabnab.htm.

[11]Lastra (2015, p. 484). For a statistical overview of the IMF resources see http://www.imf.org/external/np/tre/liquid/2015/0615.htm.

[12]The IMF "refers collectively to the various policies on the use of the Funds resources as facilities" despite the terminology being slightly imprecise, IMF review of Fund facilities—preliminary considerations, p. 3, https://www.imf.org/external/np/pdr/fac/2000/faciliti.pdf.

[13]Lastra (2015, p. 483).

accounts (Administered Accounts). Yet despite the different legal and technical nature, drawings are functionally equivalent to loans due to their 'revolving character'.[14] If a member draws on the general IMF resources, it purchases reserve currencies or SDRs from the IMF with its own currency. Similarly to loans, charges are levied on outstanding purchases and the member is obliged to re-purchase ('repay') its currency with reserve assets within a specified time period.[15]

6.2.1 Non-concessional Financing

With regard to non-concessional financing, Art. V sec. 3 a IMF Articles of Agreement differentiates between mandatory and special policies that the IMF has to or may adopt/develop to grant access to its resources. The term special refers to exceptional features of these facilities, which are either special (longer) repurchase periods under Art. V sec. 7 d IMF Articles of Agreement or special rates of charges under Art. V sec. 8 d IMF Articles of Agreement. The mandatory (normal) facilities available to members are also known as "credit tranche policies".[16] They are intended to assist short-term adjustment plans and are subject to certain conditions, which vary in intensity depending on the volume of tranche. Therefore, tranches which do not exceed 25% of the quota (in this case the IMF would hold 125% of the member's quota in the member's currency) correspond with a "first tranche conditionality" and the rest with so-called "upper credit tranches conditionality" (see below for details).[17]

Under both policy lines—mandatory and special—drawings are legally regulated by arrangements. There are four types of arrangements in total. Under the credit tranche policies these are: (1) Stand-by Arrangement (2) Flexible Credit Line (FCL) (3) Precautionary and Liquidity Line (PLL). As for special policies, the IMF developed the Extended Fund Facility (EFF) under which it grants extended arrangements and the Rapid Financing Instrument (RFI), which was introduced as a response to the global financial crisis of 2007. Arrangements are not legally binding international agreements.[18] In fact, they are not a contract at all. Arrangements are Decisions of the Executive Board of the IMF to approve a corresponding prior

---

[14]IMF (2001, p. 5).

[15]The purchase means that the IMF acquires a repurchase claim on the borrowing member, which is displayed on the asset side of the IMF balance sheet. The other member (creditor member) that provided the reserve assets for the exchange in turn acquires a claim on the IMF, called a reserve tranche position and displayed on the liability side of the balance sheet; see Lastra (2015, p. 483).

[16]Lastra (2015, p. 463); the term credit tranche is a logical consequence of the fact that IMF lending only starts once the reserve tranche has been used to the effect that the quota subscription consists fully of the member's currency.

[17]Lastra (2015, p. 463).

[18]Executive Board, Decision No. 12864-(02/102), 9/25/2002, as amended by Decision No. 13814-(06/98), 11/15/2006, para. 9.

request by member states (Art. V sec. 3 c IMF Articles of Agreement). The request is made through a letter of intent, outlining the need for assistance and an adjustment program (Art. V sec. 3 b (ii) IMF Articles of Agreement). The Decision confirms the right of the member to purchase reserve currencies or SDRs from the General Resource Account (GRA) of the IMF up to a certain amount for a certain period of time (usually 12 to 18, maximum 36 months[19]; exception: extended arrangements), given that the member meets the terms set out in the Decision.

6.2.2 Concessional Financing

As for concessional lending, the IMF has used its power under Art. V sec. 2 b IMF Articles of Agreement to focus on the needs and problems of low-income member states. Note, however, that the IMF is not a development organization but a monetary institution. Accordingly, the rationale behind using this extraordinary and in some ways more flexible instrument has to be a monetary one; namely to address the specific needs of low-income developing countries, which often lack access to private international capital markets and thus face very different circumstances than developed countries do.[20] Concessional financial assistance is disbursed via loans, not purchase/repurchase arrangements.[21]

6.3 Modalities of and Access to IMF Facilities

The resources of the IMF are finite and exist to the benefit of all its members. Consequently, it is essential that the IMF manages its financial means in a sustainable way and consistent with the purposes laid out in the charter (see "adequate safeguards" Art. I (v) and V sec. 3 a IMF Articles of Agreement).[22] Additionally, the Fund is obliged to strictly observe the principle of uniform treatment when discharging its resources. With regard to the underlying quota system, uniform treatment in the realm of financial assistance can, however, only mean proportional treatment according to quota. As for the safeguards, the approach is a two-tiered one. There are on the one hand absolute access limits preventing an excessive (over-)use of the IMF resources by any single member. On the other hand the IMF attempts to shape the modalities of its lending activity in a way that shall ensure

[19]Executive Board, Decision No. 12865-(02/102), 9/25/02, https://www.imf.org/External/np/pdr/cond/2002/eng/guid/092302.pdf.

[20]Lastra (2015, p. 484).

[21]A list of available facilities under concessional lending can be found here: http://www.imf.org/external/np/exr/facts/concesslending.htm. For a graphic overview of the IMF lending landscape see http://www.imf.org/external/np/exr/map/lending/index.htm.

[22]Lastra (2015, p. 468).

both the repayment and the structural success of the assistance. Naturally, the terms of concessional lending are more lenient than those of non-concessional lending, which is unproblematic considering the former's narrower scope in both purpose and member eligibility as well as the fact that Art. I (v) and V sec. 3 a IMF Articles of Agreement do not directly apply to concessional lending.

6.3.1 Access Limitations

Generally, all members are entitled to draw on the IMF's resources up to a specific limit expressed in a percentage of their quota. The borrowing ceiling therefore defines the scope of the member's entitlement to financial assistance (Art. V sec. 3 b (iii) IMF Articles of Agreement). Beyond that, additional financing is only available in exceptional circumstances and subject to the obtainment of a waiver by the IMF (Art. V sec. 4 IMF Articles of the Agreement). The ceiling differs depending on the category of financial assistance involved. Non-concessional financing is granted up to a limit of annually 200% of the respective quota and to a cumulative total of 600% of the quota. Concessional facilities on the other hand are capped at a volume of 150% annually and a total amount of 450%.

6.3.2 Modalities of IMF Facilities

Aside from the absolute numbers, Art. V sec. 3 b IMF Articles of Agreement requires each member who wishes to draw on the general resources of the IMF (non-concessional financing) (1) to make a representation stating the need for the assistance, (2) to be eligible to do so (Art. IV sec. 1; V sec. 5; XXVI sec. 2 IMF Articles of Agreement) and (3) to do so only in accordance with the charter and the policies adopted under it. It is common policy of the IMF not to contest a member's representation of need for financial assistance.[23]

6.3.3 Conditionality

None of these rather broad (borrowing ceiling) or soft (Art. V sec. 3 requirements) tools are the safeguards the IMF really relies on today. Instead, the IMF's resource

[23]Executive Board, Decision No. 12865-(02/102), 9/25/02, https://www.imf.org/External/np/pdr/cond/2002/eng/guid/092302.pdf.

insurance is the concept of conditionality,[24] which evolved through the life and practice of its institutions. Conditionality links the IMF financing (provision and continuation) to adjustment programs and desirable economic, fiscal or monetary targets of member states. The policies and procedures adopted under this concept thereby govern the access to and use of the financial assistance. In other words, the IMF expects member states to identify and eliminate the source of their balance of payment problem in return for the receipt and continuation of financial aid. Depending on the focus and content of the conditions, the approach can be characterized as either outcome or action based.[25] Since conditions tighten gradually the higher the credit tranche is, it is similarly possible to distinguish different types of conditionality based on their degree of strictness (hard and soft conditionality or also known as first and upper tranche conditionality).[26] A new category was introduced in the course of the last financial crisis, namely ex-ante as opposed to the normal ex-post conditionality.[27]

6.3.3.1 The Legal Base for Conditionality

The practical significance of conditionality is not reflected in the legal language of the Fund's charter. One searches in vain for a direct reference or precise legal contours of the concept.[28] It is very much a dynamic concept derived solely from the decisions and guidelines adopted by the Executive Board in order to fulfil its duty to provide temporary financial assistance consistent with the Articles of Agreement. The legal basis for this approach is entrenched in Art. V sec. 3 a and I (v) IMF Articles of Agreement. Both norms neither specify the manner nor the means applicable to ensure the sustainability of IMF lending; they merely impose a rather vague duty upon the IMF and authorize it to act accordingly.[29] The authorization basically amounts to a conferral of full discretionary powers with respect to safeguarding IMF resources and leaves ample room for the Fund to develop, expand and adapt its procedural requirements without any clear legal restrictions or limitations as long as they serve to protect the sustainability of the IMF's funds.[30] Accordingly, the concept was first foreshadowed by two early Executive Board

[24]See https://www.imf.org/external/np/exr/facts/conditio.htm.

[25]Executive Board, Decision No. 12864-(02/102), 9/25/02, as amended, para. 7 (c), https://www.imf.org/External/np/pdr/cond/2002/eng/guid/092302.pdf.

[26]Lastra (2015, pp. 464 and 481).

[27]Ex-ante means a rigorous pre-qualification process, which, once passed, allows for prompt and relatively unconditional financing. The Flexible Credit Line (FCL) is an example of ex-ante conditionality. See Lastra (2015, p. 475).

[28]Keynes and White disagreed significantly on the issue. The former strongly advocated free access to liquidity while the latter clearly favored conditional access. See Lastra (2015, p. 469).

[29]Gold (1979, p. 2).

[30]Gianviti (1999, p. 56).

Decisions mentioning the need for conditions in stand-by arrangements.[31] It was later fully developed as an independent concept by the 1964 IMF Annual Report and another Executive Board Decision in 1968 issuing the first guidelines on conditionality.[32] Since then, the concept has been continuously revised and adjusted.[33] As it originated from Executive Board Decisions, it remains under the control of this institution and can theoretically be repealed or amended by a new Decision at any time.[34]

6.3.3.2 The Rationale and Critique of Conditionality

A key component of conditionality is the practice of phasing out, i.e. disbursing credit tranches in instalments rather than in one lump sum. It is this strategy that makes the conditions set out in an arrangement effective tools in enforcing member states' compliance with their IMF obligations. It also illustrates the rationale behind conditionality. Aside from channelling the access to IMF resources, it also performs a "carrot and stick" function, which has equally important side effects such as strengthening the credibility of the adjustment program among private investors and reducing moral hazard effects resulting from the availability of financial aid.[35]

Despite the noble goals of conditionality, the concept has a rather negative connotation these days. The critical perception stems largely from accusations that the IMF uses conditionality to undermine state sovereignty and democratic processes. The critique is not entirely unfounded. The combination of broad discretionary powers and the complexity and interplay of monetary, economic and fiscal policies responsible for the balance of payment problems led to a considerable expansion of national policies covered by conditionality. Via the link of necessary fiscal adjustments the IMF began to become involved with topics which lie well outside the scope of its core expertise (e.g. privatisation, social security reform) and maybe even mandate. An aggravating factor was the excessively detailed monitoring process, effectively resulting in micromanaging the program implementation at national level.[36] The critique was, however, taken very seriously. In response to the allegations, a thorough revision of the guidelines concluded that the concept of conditionality had to be realigned to serve the following principles: (1) National ownership (of the adjustment program) and transparency; (2) parsimony in

[31]Executive Board, Decision No. 284-4, 3/10/1948, and Decision No. 102-(52/11). 2/13/1952.

[32]Executive Board, Decision No. 2603-(68/132), 9/20/1968.

[33]Important milestones were the Executive Board Decisions of 1979 (No. 6056-(79/38)); 2002 (No. 12864-(02/102)) and consistently updated 'Operational Guidelines' issued to IMF staff since 2003, see for the latest (2014) https://www.imf.org/external/np/pp/eng/2014/072314.pdf.

[34]Lastra (2015, p. 472).

[35]See Lastra (2015, p. 472 s).

[36]For a detailed overview of the critique directed at conditionality see Lastra (2015, p. 474 ss).

conditions; (3) clarity of conditions (scope and content); (4) tailored to the needs of each individual member state (but in accordance with the principle of uniform treatment)[37] and (5) effective coordination with other organizations and creditors (to avoid duplication and provide for coherent conditions).[38]

6.3.3.3 Conditionality in Practice

In practice, the conditions are drawn from the member state's request for financial assistance. Generally, such a request consists of the formal demand and a letter of intent (LOI) or a memorandum of economic and financial policies (MEFP) outlining the member's reform plan/program. The LOI or MEFP are sometimes accompanied by a technical memorandum of understanding (TMU). Two things should be borne in mind: The LOI/MEFP is a unilateral commitment to adjust and not an acceptance of international enforceable obligations. Furthermore, it is the member state that is solely responsible for the design, details and focus of the adjustment program (national ownership). The arrangement is a (response-)decision of the Fund and the conditions set out there are simply elements of the proposed program the IMF regards as particularly significant. However, in reality national ownership sometimes becomes a rather fictional term. Member states are acutely aware of what kind of programs the IMF approves of through the annual consultation process and are keen to cater to the preferences of the IMF in order to secure funding (known as the "Washington consensus").[39] Once effective, the arrangement and particularly the conditions therein form the basis for the monitoring of the member state's performance. The performance is assessed through performance criteria (specific variables and measures), program review (usually every six months), prior actions (i.e. before assistance gets approved or before completion of a review) and indicative targets as well as structural benchmarks (the latter two comprise uncertain or vague variables and failure to comply does not per se intercept the financing).[40] Similar to the surveillance function, information plays a key role here as well. Member states are obliged to furnish accurate information to the IMF (Art. Art. VIII sec 5 IMF Articles of Agreement) and a failure to do so or a misrepresentation may lead to sanctions (Art XXVI IMF Articles of Agreement). It is this combination of expertise, knowledge and financial resources which makes the IMF a powerful international organization despite the sometimes soft terms of its charter.

[37] Uniform treatment does not mean equal treatment regardless of the circumstances but rather equal treatment of similar cases.

[38] Lastra (2015, p. 479).

[39] Lastra (2015, p. 477).

[40] Lastra (2015, p. 478 s).

6.4 Crisis Management

A few remarks may be made on the IMF's role in (financial) crisis management[41] due to the topicality of the subject but also due to the increased portfolio of financial tasks the IMF has assumed over the past decades.[42] First, it is important to bear in mind that while the history of sovereign debt has so far consistently also been one of sovereign debt crisis, the IMF is not designed nor equipped for the long-term financing of unsustainable debt burdens (finite resources, purposes of the IMF see Art. I IMF Articles of Agreement). Hence, any involvement of the IMF is subject to a debt sustainability analysis (DSA)[43] and the provisions set out in the charter. The IMF enjoys a de facto or customary preferred creditor status, which originally began because the lending activity is not of a commercial nature but serves other purposes (see Art. I IMF Articles of Agreement) and is not aimed at generating profit. Moreover, it is also a way of compensating the IMF for often providing financial assistance when no one else still would. Ironically, the only written legal reference to the IMF preferred creditor status can be found in the ESM treaty, which simply premises the existence of the status (recital 13: "(…) ESM loans will enjoy preferred creditor status in a similar fashion to those of the IMF (…)"). In the past, private creditors usually welcomed the involvement of the IMF despite the preferred creditor status because they were keen on benefitting from the implicit effects of the IMF conditionality (third party beneficiaries).[44] Given its unique position—relations to both the creditor and debtor country—the Fund often acts as an honest broker between the parties in debt restructuring negotiations. To this end, the IMF devised a strategy of burden sharing among private and public creditors which aims to divide the burden equitably.[45] Ultimately, its past involvement in crisis management also earned the IMF a reputation as international lender of last resort. Comparable to commercial banks turning to their central banks if money is no longer available on acceptable terms elsewhere,[46] governments or central banks turn to the IMF if foreign currencies are no longer available elsewhere on acceptable terms. The IMF should be very cautious though in taking on this particular role, since it lacks a central bank's capability of creating money. Moreover, issues like moral hazard effects, symmetrical treatment of members (interventions of this sort normally consume considerable amounts of the resources) and last but not least the preservation of the credibility of the IMF (decisive for its work and preferred creditor status) need to be considered carefully.[47]

---

[41]See https://www.imf.org/external/np/exr/facts/changing.htm.

[42]For a detailed analysis of the subject see Lastra (2015, p. 524 ss).

[43]See http://www.imf.org/external/np/pp/eng/2013/050913.pdf.

[44]Lastra (2015, p. 534). The assessment is not necessarily true today since financing patterns shifted from loans (commercial banks) to bonds (private citizens).

[45]Lastra (2015, p. 536 s).

[46]On the lender of last resort function of central banks see Lastra (2015, p. 45 ss).

[47]See Lastra (2015, p. 542 s).

6.5 The IMF and Currency Unions

Frist things first: What is a currency union? The IMF defines currency unions as "*agreement(s) among members of that union (countries or other jurisdictions) to share a common currency, and a single monetary and foreign exchange policy*".[48] This correctly excludes mere exchange-rate regime choices, e.g. Dollarization, dual legal tender arrangements, from being characterized as currency unions solely by virtue of sharing a currency.[49] Besides the Euro area there are currently three other currency unions: Two African (Central African Monetary Union and West African Monetary Union) and one Caribbean (Eastern Caribbean Monetary Union).[50]

6.5.1 IMF Membership

The main issue arising from the IMF legal framework when dealing with currency unions is membership. Art. II sec. 2 IMF Articles of Agreement states in clear terms that membership is only open to countries. Now it is undisputed that (so far) none of the unions mentioned above have reached a level of integration that would equal statehood. *Smits* nevertheless argues that the EU (formerly the Community) features all characteristics of "*countries*" for the purposes of the IMF and Art. II sec. 2 IMF Articles of Agreement should therefore be interpreted accordingly.[51] The majority reading of Art. II sec. 2 is, however, that countries under international law are only those entities that have a defined territory, a permanent population and the competence to create competences for themselves, which the EU does not have.[52] Consequently, currency unions are banned from becoming official members of the IMF under the current setting of the charter; any change would require a formal amendment of the membership provision.

6.5.2 The IMF and Currency Unions in Practice

Notwithstanding the legal indifference of the Articles of Agreements vis-à-vis currency unions, it is not feasible for the IMF to ignore the realities created by regional monetary integration. The existence of currency unions indeed has significant implications for the work of the Fund as may be illustrated by the IMF's

[48]CUTEG (2004), para. 1.

[49]See also Proctor (2005, p. 624 s).

[50]Proctor (2012, p. 672 ss).

[51]Smits (1997, p. 442 ss).

[52]Zilioli and Selmayer (2001, p. 235), Lastra (2015, p. 352); The EU's territory is that of its member states, so is its population and it does not possess the competence to create competences.

approach to the Euro area[53]: (1) Surveillance: While the IMF continues its consultations with each individual member state (Art. IV IMF Articles of Agreement), the process now involves representatives of the relevant EU institutions as well, taking into account the EU competences in monetary matters and the regional perspective regarding fiscal and economic policies. Additionally, the IMF conducts separate annual consultations with the Euro area as a whole.[54] (2) SDRs: The value of SDRs is calculated on the basis of a currency basket. The Deutsche Mark and the French Franc were replaced by the Euro in the currency basket upon the beginning of EMU. (3) Holding and management of foreign reserves: Art. 31 ESCB Statute allows Euro area member states to use their remaining residual amount of reserve assets (after the transfer of a certain amount to the ECB pursuant to Art. 30 sec. 1 ESCB Statute) to fulfil their obligation with the IMF. Furthermore, it subjects any other reserve asset transaction beyond a certain limit to the approval of the ECB. Additionally, Art. 30 sec. 5 ESCB Statute authorizes the ECB to hold and manage IMF reserve positions and SDRs. Finally, the ECB was granted an observer status by the IMF to the effect that the ECB is allowed to send a representative to certain Executive Board Meetings which are of special interest to the ECB.[55]

References

CUTEG (2004) Definition of currency union. https://www.imf.org/external/np/sta/bop/pdf/cuteg1.pdf

Gianviti F (1999) Decision making in the IMF. Current developments in monetary and financial law, vol 1. IMF, Washington, pp 31–67

Gold J (1979) Conditionality. IMF Pamphlet series No. 31. IMF, Washington

IMF (2001) Financial organization and operations of the IMF, Pamphlet series No. 45, 6th edition 2001, IMF, Washington https://www.imf.org/external/pubs/ft/pam/pam45/pdf/pam45.pdf

IMF (2014) IMF financial operations 2014. http://www.imf.org/external/pubs/ft/finop/2014/index.htm

Lastra R (2015) International financial and monetary law, 2nd edn. Oxford University Press, Oxford

Proctor C (2005) Mann on the legal aspects of money, 6th edn. Oxford University Press, Oxford

Proctor C (2012) Mann on the legal aspects of money, 7th edn. Oxford University Press, Oxford

Smits R (1997) The European Central Bank, institutional aspects, 1st edn. Kluwer Law International, The Hague

Zilioli C, Selmayer M (2001) The law of the European Central Bank, 1st edn. Hart Publishing, Oxford

[53]See http://www.imf.org/external/np/exr/facts/europe.htm.

[54]IMF, 2015 Article IV Consultation with the Euro Area Concluding Statement of IMF Mission http://www.imf.org/external/np/ms/2015/061815.htm.

[55]IMF, Press Release No. 98/64, 12/22/1998, https://www.imf.org/external/np/sec/pr/1998/pr9864.htm.

Chapter 7
History of European Monetary Law

7.1 The Historical Development of the European Monetary Constitution

The history of the European Union (EU) and in particular of economic and monetary integration is not a story of linear evolution according to an ideal abstract system, but one shaped by events and political will, by trial and error, by successes and failures. Moreover, it should not be perceived as a development independent from international monetary cooperation, but rather as one linked to it.[1] Particularly since the aftermath of the World War II, the creation of a stable monetary system was widely believed to be a viable mean to foster peace and prosperity.[2] States have, however, varied their approaches toward this goal—often in reaction to certain events—from global to regional strategies. It is therefore no coincidence that the real push for regional monetary integration in Europe followed after the breakdown of the Bretton Woods par-value system.[3] In other words, both forms of cooperation deal with similar issues, albeit in different contexts and with different legal set-ups. The EMU project always also served broader European integrational processes, goes far beyond mere cooperation today and has a greater political dimension to it than the IMF system.

[1]See Lastra (2015, p. 221).

[2]In this context see Art. 2 of the Treaty Establishing the European Economic Communities (known as Treaty of Rome).

[3]Lastra (2015, p. 221); although, as Lastra notes as well, the Werner Report predates the collapse of the par-value system. The observation is therefore not entirely chronologically accurate but nonetheless overall correct.

C. Herrmann and C. Dornacher, *International and European Monetary Law*,
SpringerBriefs in Law, DOI 10.1007/978-3-319-57642-8_7

7.1.1 *First Initiatives of Multilateral Monetary Cooperation in Europe*

7.1.1.1 The European Payments Union

The initial momentum for the commencement of multilateral monetary cooperation in Europe was triggered by very practical considerations after World War II. The lack of multilateral payments systems impeded trade in goods and services and thus the reconstruction and recovery efforts of war-torn European economies. The approximately 200 bilateral payment agreements in place at the time proved ineffective to accommodate these needs as bilateral balance of payment equilibria were still necessary and simultaneously impossible to achieve in practice.[4] Therefore, the treaty on the establishment of the Organisation for European Economic Cooperation (OEEC),[5] which would become responsible for the distribution of the Marshall Plan[6] funds, contained a provision for the introduction of a multilateral payments system (Art. 4 OEEC Treaty). This provision was anticipated in part by the first clearing arrangements in 1947/48 and became fully implemented upon the creation of the European Payments Union (EPU) in 1950. The EPU presented a mechanism for settling payments amongst participating European countries and was operated by the BIS, which acted as an agent for the OEEC.[7] The mechanism provided for a monthly balancing of all the EPU members' reciprocal assets and liabilities in the balance sheets of the respective central banks by allowing, for example, France to use a credit balance generated through a trade surplus vis-à-vis Italy to settle their deficit with the United Kingdom. The settlement was additionally supported by gold and Dollar funds from the Marshall Plan to address peak imbalances. The creation of the EPU ultimately contributed towards full convertibility of members' currencies, which was de facto achieved in 1958 and legally in 1961 on formal acceptance of Art. VIII IMF Articles of Agreement. It also greatly assisted the economic reconstruction and recovery efforts.[8] The EPU ceased to exist in 1959 as it was replaced by the European Monetary Agreement, which absorbed its functions and remained active until the 1970s.

---

[4]Herrmann (2010, p. 195 ss).

[5]The OEEC was established in 1948 to manage the Marshall Plan funds and was later succeeded by the Organization for Economic Cooperation and Development (OECD)—a world-wide body—after its objectives had been mostly achieved in 1961, see Lastra (2015, p. 222) and http://www.oecd.org/general/organisationforeuropeaneconomicco-operation.htm.

[6]The name Marshall Plan goes back to the US Secretary of State George Marshall, who announced the "European Recovery Program" in his famous Harvard speech in June 1947, for more information see http://marshallfoundation.org/marshall/the-marshall-plan/.

[7]Lastra (2015, p. 222).

[8]Lastra (2015, p. 222).

7.1.1.2 The EEC Treaty

When in 1957 Belgium, France, Italy, Luxembourg, the Netherlands and West Germany embarked on a journey towards economic policy coordination[9] and integrating markets by signing the Treaty of Rome Establishing the European Economic Community (The EEC Treaty), monetary policy was not on the agenda. The monetary references in the treaty were rudimentary, intergovernmental in content and without any direct effect, rendering them unenforceable for private citizens.[10] Considering the interdependence of economic and monetary policies this may seem awkward, yet, it actually solely evidences the strong reliance of the treaty drafters on the IMF par-value system.[11] During the negotiations for the EEC Treaty, "Bretton Woods" was still a functioning monetary regime, providing for stable international monetary relations.[12] Moreover, the economic reality of the 1950ies, shaped by industrial and agricultural production instead of financial services, did not automatically require addressing the concept of money in greater depth.[13] It was therefore sufficient to aim for current and capital account convertibility to the extent necessary for the newly established common market to function (emphasis lay on current account convertibility, cf. Art. 106 EEC Treaty; Art. VIII sec. 2 IMF Articles of Agreement). With regard to future institutional developments, Art. 105 EEC Treaty is nonetheless of interest as it introduced the idea of institutionalizing monetary cooperation.[14] Based on this provision, the advisory Monetary Committee[15] (1958) and the Committee of Governors of Central Banks of the Member States of the European Economic Community[16] (1964) were established. The latter, designed as a forum for central bank coordination, gradually gained in importance and later on played a major role in preparing the ESCB Statute, which governs the life and work of the ECB and the European System of Central Banks today.[17]

---

[9]Smits notes, however, that the coordination mechanisms never really came to life partly due to political reasons and partly due to the lack of material ('hard') norms in this respect, Smits (1997, p. 12).

[10]This is in contrast to the common market integration process, which was significantly moved forward by the European Court of Justice's (ECJ) judicial intervention, see Lastra (2015, p. 224).

[11]Smits (1997, p. 10 ss).

[12]See also The Economist (1998).

[13]Smits (1997, p. 10).

[14]Lastra (2015, p. 224).

[15]The Monetary Committee existed until the beginning of the third stage of EMU and was subsequently replaced by the Economic and Financial Committee, Art. 134 TFEU.

[16]See Council Decision 64/300/EEC, 8.05.1964, OJ 1964 p. 1206; it ceased to exist at the beginning of the second stage of EMU; the European Monetary Institute (EMI) took over its role.

[17]Smits (1997, p. 13), Scheller and ECB (2004, p. 17).

7.1.2 Monetary Implications of the European Integration Process

Even though the EEC Treaty largely ignored the monetary question, the reality it brought into being nonetheless had some profound effects on the path of the European monetary agenda. The establishment of the customs union (Art. 3 a) and b), 9 para. 1 ECC Treaty) and based on that the creation of the common market (Art. 2 ECC Treaty) offered some fresh impetus for the idea of European monetary cooperation.[18] The reasons are threefold: (1) Quite fundamentally for the envisaged economic approximation, a parallel liberalization of payment flows was indispensable.[19] Related to this, the increase in intra-European trade volume and relations also drew a greater focus on the exchange-rates between participating currencies. National monetary policies, aimed at generating competitive trade advantages, threatened the integration project in a similar fashion as the common market undermined the effectiveness of national economic policies in the reverse direction.[20] The motive for cooperation in this scenario became "to regain collectively what states would lose individually".[21] (2) Furthermore, the use of fundamental freedoms by citizens influenced current accounts and consequentially affected the balance of payments of the member states. (3) Finally, the operation of several Community policies depended upon a common store of value and unit of account, e.g. the common agricultural policy, customs policies and last but not least the Community's budget.[22] Unsurprisingly, the Commission concluded already in 1962 that a customs union would inevitably lead to an economic and monetary union (the Marjolin Memorandum).[23] However, the monetary implications of the European integration process did not become fully visible until the stability of the Bretton Woods par-value system suffered fractures by the late 1960ies. The changed international environment caused monetary disturbances and a resurgence of economic policies driven by national interests, which in turn threatened to disrupt the European integration project.[24] In this context, the Commission began to actively support the idea of EMU by submitting the so-called 'Barre Plan'[25] to the Council.[26] The plan formed the basis for the '*Werner Plan*' (see below), which marked the shift from pursuing (mere) monetary cooperation to aiming at monetary integration in Europe.

---

[18]Herrmann (2010, p. 198).

[19]Lastra (2015, p. 223).

[20]Herrmann (2010, p. 198), Smits (1997, p. 11 s).

[21]Smits (1997, p. 12), although Smits only referred to economic cooperation with this statement, it nonetheless also applies to monetary cooperation.

[22]Smits (1997, p. 14).

[23]Scheller and ECB (2004, p. 17).

[24]Scheller and ECB (2004, p. 17).

[25]Available at http://aei.pitt.edu/1091/1/Barr_Plan_II_COM__70_300.pdf.

[26]Smits (1997, p. 13).

7.1.3 *The Evolution of the European Economic and Monetary Union*

The idea of an economic and monetary union did not just emerge with the beginning demise of the Bretton Woods regime;[27] it had been around in different shapes and forms for a while, but it did transform a visionary idea into a potentially politically feasible option. Nevertheless, the road toward EMU still proved to be a cumbersome one.

7.1.3.1 The Werner Report

The Werner Report[28] is the final report on a study of options for an economic and monetary union, submitted in October 1970. The study was commissioned by the Heads of State or Governments of the EEC countries at The Hague conference in December 1969 following the Barre Report. The report suggested establishing an economic and monetary union within ten years according to a three-stage plan. The recommendations also included to fully liberalize capital movement, permanently lock the exchange-rates between member state currencies and ultimately to introduce a common currency.[29] With regard to the economic element of the union, the report emphasised strengthening economic policy coordination and suggested relatively far-reaching Community competences in the public budget domain (determination of volume, size of balances and methods of financing).[30] The report did not propose a detailed institutional arrangement for EMU, but concluded that the creation of a Community central banking system and a centre of decision of economic policy would be mandatory.[31] Despite approving of the principal message of the report, the six member states were unable to agree on some of the crucial points contained therein. Ultimately, the Council and the representatives of the governments of the member states adopted a resolution, known as the '1971 EMU Resolution', launching the first stage on a trial basis. The attempt was to narrow currency fluctuation margins ('the snake' see below) and to create a European Fund for monetary cooperation, which was meant to be a precursor for the Community system of central banks.[32] Diverging policy responses to the economic shocks of the decade (e.g. 1973 oil crisis) and the fallout of the collapse of the Bretton Woods regime significantly slowed down the political momentum by the mid-1970ies,

---

[27] J. Monet, for example, had already proposed a European Reserve Fund in the late 1950ies, see Smits (1997, p. 12).

[28] Available at http://aei.pitt.edu/1002/1/monetary_werner_final.pdf.

[29] Lastra (2015, p. 225).

[30] Werner (1970, p. 12).

[31] Werner (1970, p. 12).

[32] Lastra (2015, p. 225 s).

which thwarted the attempt in the end and caused the plan to fail—it was officially abandoned in December 1974.[33]

7.1.3.2 The 'Snake in the Tunnel'

Before the Werner Plan inspired three-stage EMU plan unravelled, the six member states tried to align their exchange-rate policies in order to avoid intra-Community exchange-rate volatility, which had been identified to impede trade and threaten common policies. The measure of choice was a mechanism of managed block floating. It allowed the member states' currencies ('the snake') to float within specified margins of fluctuation against the Dollar ('the tunnel'), hence the name 'snake in the tunnel'.[34] Currency fluctuations were to be maintained within 0.75% vis-à-vis the Dollar so as to limit the bilateral fluctuation between member state currencies to max. 1.5%. Due to reasons explained above, 'the snake' ended up being a short-lived experiment, losing most of its members in less than two years and eventually shrunk to a 'mark area' encompassing only West Germany, the Benelux countries and Denmark.[35]

7.1.3.3 The European Monetary Cooperation Fund

The European Monetary Cooperation Fund (EMCF) on the other hand never lived up to its name as member states were extremely reluctant to vest it with substantial functions in the field of central bank cooperation and monetary policy. The reluctance possibly resulted from the legal source of the EMCF—a Council regulation,[36] which put it under the regulatory control of Community institutions.[37] Consequently, the EMCF fulfilled solely technical functions in connection with the implementation and maintenance of 'the snake in the tunnel'.[38] Subsequently, the EMCF resumed this role for the ERM.

7.1.3.4 The European Monetary System

After the collapse of the Bretton Woods regime had sealed the fate of the Werner Plan for EMU, volatility became a defining feature of the European currencies.

---

[33]Scheller and ECB (2004, p. 18), Lastra (2015, p. 227).

[34]Resolution of the Council and of the Representatives of the Governments of the Member States of 21 March 1972 on the application of the Resolution of 21 March 1971 on the attainment by stages of economic and monetary union in the Community, OJ C 38/3 (18 April 1972).

[35]Scheller and ECB (2004, p. 18).

[36]See Council Regulation (EEC) No 907/73 of 3 April 1973 establishing a European Monetary Cooperation Fund, OJ L 89/2 (5 April 1973).

[37]Scheller and ECB (2004, p. 18).

[38]Lastra (2015, p. 226 s).

Attempting to replace the lost external anchor that was provided by the par-value system, the German-Franco alliance ('the engine of European integration) proposed a 'zone of monetary stability in Europe'. This zone—the European Monetary System—was designed to be an institutional arrangement pursuing stable exchange-rates, price stability and paving the way for a monetary union through cooperation.[39] Regardless of its rather fragile legal foundation, a Council resolution and a procedural framework based on an Agreement of the EC central banks, the EMS lived up to expectations and remained the primary monetary cooperation arrangement until the creation of EMU.[40] The approach of the EMS was twofold: It introduced the European Currency Unit (ECU) and provided an exchange-rate and intervention mechanism (ERM), which served as a successor to 'the snake'. The ECU was never legal tender, but functioned as unit of account at EC level, as a means of payment between monetary authorities in the Community and as a reserve asset for central banks. Its value was based on a currency basket containing all member state currencies.[41] The similarities to its contemporary, the IMF's SDR, are fairly obvious. The ERM represents a system of fixed but adjustable exchange-rates and roughly follows the same principle that governed 'the snake in the tunnel', yet without aiming at a certain exchange-rate vis-à-vis the US Dollar. The mechanism was, however, significantly modified, reducing the flaws of 'the snake' and designed to be a parity grid of bilateral exchange-rates with pre-announced floors and ceilings.[42] Essentially, the ECU served as the anchor of the system in the sense that all participating currencies were convertible into ECU, which in turn resulted in the existence of cross-exchange-rates amongst member state currencies. The central banks were committed to intervene, keeping the currency fluctuations within a specified margin of ±2.25% (6% in the early phase of ERM participation) amongst each other.[43] Despite its practical 'failure' in 1992/93 under speculative attacks, which drove the UK and Italy to exit the mechanism and widened the fluctuation band from ±2.25 to 15%, membership in the ERM was included in two out of four economic convergence criteria by the Maastricht Treaty. In fact, it remains effective to this day, albeit in a revised version (ERM II), serving as exchange-rate mechanism between the Euro and the member states' currencies that are not yet participating in the Euro area.[44]

[39]Lastra (2015, p. 228).

[40]Lastra (2015, p. 228).

[41]Lastra (2015, p. 228). The basket was eventually frozen on August 1st 1994, Art. 118 EC Treaty (post Maastricht).

[42]Smits (1997, p. 21).

[43]Lastra (2015, p. 228).

[44]Lastra (2015, p. 229).

7.1.3.5 The Delors Report

Capitalizing on the momentum for integration generated by the adoption of the Single European Act,[45] the credo once again became 'one market needs one money' in the 1980ies.[46] It also coincided with warnings of economists that free trade, free movement of capital, fixed exchange-rates and independent national monetary policies were mutually inconsistent (see Chap. 3). The renewed approach to establishing a monetary union followed familiar patterns: A study of possible options was commissioned in June 1988 by the Hanover European Council (Delors Committee), which concluded in a final report—the Delors Report.[47] The report picked up the Werner report idea of a phased establishment process for the EMU (three stages) and proposed an institutional arrangement centred on the European System of Central Banks (ESCB). It is probably safe to say that the Delors report is the intellectual 'creator' of the EMU that subsequently materialized through the Maastricht Treaty.

7.1.3.6 The Maastricht Treaty

The idea of EMU finally received a legal base and was implemented through the Treaty on the European Union (Maastricht Treaty), adopted by the Council in December 1991 and signed on February 7 1992. The 'triumph' did not come without a cost though. As mentioned above, EMU is not shaped according to a single coherent abstract idea but is the product of diverse interests and a continuing political struggle for the national and common good. The Maastricht Treaty is a prime example in this regard of a compromise struck between forces favouring a federal Europe and those who seek to reaffirm national sovereignty; a compromise, which is reflected in the ambiguity of many treaty provisions.[48] Furthermore, some of the commitments and objectives of the European monetary institutions, which will be discussed later on, root in the underlying monetary stability culture that prevails in Europe.[49] With regard to legal technicalities, the Maastricht Treaty constituted an extensive amendment to the EC Treaty framework and fully endorsed the three-stage proposal of the Delors report. Therefore, the phased establishment of EMU began in 1990 and stage three is underway since January 1st 1999. In particular the three stages were/are:

---

[45]Eur-Lex, The Single European Act, http://eur-lex.europa.eu/legal-content/EN/TXT/?uri=uriserv:xy0027.

[46]See Commission (1990) http://ec.europa.eu/economy_finance/publications/pages/publication7454_en.pdf.

[47]Available at http://aei.pitt.edu/1007/1/monetary_delors.pdf.

[48]Lastra (2015, p. 232).

[49]Lastra (2015, p. 232).

Stage one (from July 1st until December 31st 1993)[50]: The first stage laid the groundwork for the envisaged unification and thus focused on liberalizing capital flows, aiming for the free movement of capital between member states. Additionally, member states were required to review domestic laws regarding the access of governments and other public authorities to central bank financing as well as to privileged conditions from financial institutions (Art. 101, 102 and 116 EC Treaty; now Art. 123, 124 and 139 TFEU). Moreover, economic policy making was to be coordinated with the Council and exchange-rate policies were to be conducted in the interest of the Community.

Stage two (from January 1st 1994 until December 31st 1998)[51]: The transition to stage two did not depend on formal decisions or specific results in stage one. The main goals of stage two were to achieve greater economic convergence among member states and reformation of the national central banks in preparation for the ESCB. To this end, several convergence programs were launched and member states were expected to (1) avoid excessive budget deficits (Art. 104 EC Treaty, now Art. 126 TFEU), (2) revise their national law in accordance with the Treaty and the ESCB Statute, in particular the independence of their national central banks (Art. 108, 109 EC Treaty, now Art. 130, 131 TFEU) and (3) make significant progress on fulfilling the four convergence criteria (price stability, sustainable public budgets, exchange-rate stability within ERM, low long-term interest rate levels), which are a precondition for the move to the third and last stage (Art. 121 EC Treaty, now Art. 140 TFEU, see also Protocol No. 13). In preparation for the institutional transition, the European Monetary Institute (EMI) was created as a predecessor of the ESCB. It replaced the EMCF and the Committee of Central Bank Governors. On a formal, but practically very relevant note the Heads of State or Government of the member states decided to call the single currency 'Euro'.

Stage three (since January 1st 1999)[52]: The last stage—the completion of EMU—began with eleven initial members (Belgium, Germany, Spain, France, Ireland, Italy, Luxembourg, the Netherlands, Austria, Portugal and Finland), who had fulfilled the four convergence criteria by then. The UK and Denmark obtained so-called opt-out clauses exempting them from participation in stage three regardless of their convergence level (see Protocols 15 and 16).[53] After the determination and irrevocable fixing of exchange-rates in 1998/1999, the Euro became the single currency of the Euro area, abolishing and substituting national currencies.[54] Simultaneously, the ECB and the ESCB assumed their full powers and responsibility for the single currency and monetary policy. It was not until January

[50]Lastra (2015, p. 233 s).

[51]Lastra (2015, p. 234 ss).

[52]Lastra (2015, p. 236 s).

[53]Conversely, Sweden does not possess a formal opt-out status but achieved a temporary derogation status by purposefully not complying with several convergence criteria.

[54]Technically, the ECU was transformed from a composite currency, whose value depended on the currency basket, into an independent currency.

1st 2002, however, that the Euro should become a tangible reality for the Euro area citizens with the introduction of Euro banknotes and coins and the beginning of the cash changeover. Since the advent of stage three, another eight member states have joined the Euro area, which now encompasses nineteen countries.[55]

The preceding historical outline began with the assertion that Economic and Monetary Union is a reality today. This is only entirely accurate in terms of the Monetary Union. Conversely, the Economic Union basically boils down to policy coordination with member states retaining important sovereign powers, e.g. substantial control over fiscal policies.[56] This asymmetrical constitution of EMU has often been criticized and proved to play a decisive role during the European sovereign debt crisis (see Chaps. 13 and 14). Despite the recent crisis-induced significant developments, the expectation that the early move toward monetary unification would eventually entail an economic unification did not materialize. Much like in the aftermath of the par-value collapse, the natural instinct of member states seems to be a retreat to national sentiments and a display of sovereignty reflexes. In conclusion, the road to Economic and Monetary Union remains an ongoing integration process with a not yet foreseeable concrete outcome.

References

Herrmann C (2010) Währungshoheit, Währungsverfassung und subjektive Rechte, 1st edn. Mohr Siebeck, Thübingen

Lastra R (2015) International financial and monetary law, 2nd edn. Oxford University Press, Oxford

Scheller H, ECB (2004) The European Central Bank—history, role and functions. ECB, Frankfurt am Main. https://www.ecb.europa.eu/pub/pdf/other/ecbhistoryrolefunctions2004en.pdf

Smits R (1997) The European Central Bank, institutional aspects, 1st edn. Kluwer Law International, The Hague

The Economist (1998) EMU the history of an idea. The Economist. http://www.economist.com/node/159451

Werner P (1970) Report to the council and the commission on the realization by stages of EMU in the community. http://aei.pitt.edu/1002/1/monetary_werner_final.pdf

[55]European Commission, What is the Euro?, http://ec.europa.eu/economy_finance/euro/adoption/euro_area/index_en.htm.

[56]Lastra (2015, p. 241).

Chapter 8
The Legal Framework of EMU post Lisbon—Institutional Setup

The European Union (EU) is often referred to as an entity "sui generis", somewhere between a mere confederation of nation states and a real federal state. This peculiarity is reflected in its legislation as well as in the design of its institutions that are more often than not based on complex, multi-layered structures. They represent the growing importance of the Union and the residual sovereignty of the member states. Naturally, the institutions' historical evolution has also left its mark on the structure and design of EMU. The result is a dual monetary/economic construct with a decentralized central banking system (the National Central Banks, NCB) under the unifying/centralized 'governance' of the ECB,[1] which is primarily responsible for monetary matters, and an economic policy coordination managed by the ECOFIN Council and the Eurogroup (only Euro area Council members). Special guidance and advice is provided by the Commission and the Economic and Financial Committee, which replaced the Monetary Committee upon entry into the third stage of EMU (Art. 134 TFEU).

The institutional work aims to advance monetary integration, specifically the common currency 'Euro' (Art. 3 (4) TEU), and to pursue balanced economic growth (Art. 3 (1–3) TEU) within an open market economy, allowing for free competition (Art. 119 (1) TFEU) while maintaining economic, social and territorial cohesion and solidarity (Art. 3 (2–3) TEU). The overriding monetary principle, however, is the objective of price stability (Art. 119 (2), 127 (1) TFEU). The primary law provisions[2] relevant to EMU are scattered across both EU treaties (TEU and TFEU) and can be found in the following Articles and Protocols:

- Art. 3 (3), (4); 13 (1), (2), (3) TEU (objectives and institutions)
- Art. 3 (1) c) TFEU (monetary policy competence)
- Art. 63–66 TFEU (capital and payments)

[1]Moutot et al. (2008, p. 17).
[2]Both treaties (TEU and TFEU) as well as all Protocols are considered the primary law of the EU, i.e., the EU's "constitution". Secondary law on the other hand are directives, regulations and decisions adopted by EU institutions in accordance with primary law, i.e., derivative law.

C. Herrmann and C. Dornacher, *International and European Monetary Law*,
SpringerBriefs in Law, DOI 10.1007/978-3-319-57642-8_8

- Art. 119–144 TFEU (economic and monetary policy)
- Art. 219 TFEU (exchange-rate regime vis-à-vis non EU-member states)
- Art. 282–284 TFEU (ECB)
- ESBC/ECB Statute (Protocol No. 4)
- Protocols:

  No. 12 (excessive deficit)
  No. 13 (convergence criteria)
  No. 14 (Euro Group)
  No. 15 (UK), No. 16, 17 (Denmark)

In addition to these provisions, there are several secondary law sources governing the work and functioning of the institutions. Reference to them will be made accordingly.

8.1 ESCB and ECB

8.1.1 Institutional Design

The institutional heart of EMU is the ESCB. It is a central banking system made up of the ECB, headquartered in Frankfurt,[3] and all EU member state NCBs (currently twenty-eight[4]). The ESCB is based on a decentralized structure (the NCBs as executive branches, see Art. 12 (3) ESCB Statute)[5] with a centralized decision-making process (the ECB as 'head' of the system, see Art. 129 TFEU).[6] This particular choice of institutional design—a combination of union and national elements—may seem ordinary in an EU context, yet it bears some remarkable features. The decentralization is not just a functional one but also a very distinctive legal division. While the ECB is a creature of EU law, the NCBs are not. Notwithstanding the member states' obligation to ensure compatibility of their respective central banking laws with EU law (Art. 131 TFEU), the legal source of each NCB remains a national one with ample room for national peculiarities and preferences. Thus NCBs have a dual status: They form an integral part of the ESCB when performing tasks for the system and remain otherwise national agencies (see Art. 14 (3) ESCB Statute).[7] Moreover, another distinction can be drawn between NCBs of Euro area member states (the 'ins') and non-Euro area members (the 'outs'). Only the 'ins' together with the ECB constitute the Eurosystem (Art.

[3]Art. 1 (g) Decision of government representatives on the location of the seats of certain bodies and departments of the EC (now EU) and of Europol, OJ 1993, No. L 323/1.

[4]See http://europa.eu/about-eu/countries/member-countries/.

[5]Smits (1997, p. 112).

[6]For the rationale behind a decentralized system see Moutot et al. (2008, p. 17 ss).

[7]Smits (1997, p. 94), Lastra (2015, p. 250).

282 (1) TFEU), which is responsible for formulating the European monetary policy. Considering the policy only applies to the Euro area, the division is appropriate.

The ECB on the other hand is an official EU institution (Art. 13 TEU) with legal personality (Art. 282 (3) TFEU) and is solely based on union law. The ECB is fully capitalized by the NCBs through subscriptions, whose volume is determined by the key in Art. 29 ESCB Statute, and foreign reserve asset contributions (Art. 30 ESCB Statute) (currently the capital base is 10.8 billion Euros[8]).[9] Therefore, the only shareholders of the ECB are NCBs (Art. 28 (2) ESCB Statute).[10] They are also the recipients of the net profit, proportional to their share, accrued in the performance of ESCB monetary functions by NCBs (Art. 32 (5) ESCB Statute) or the ECB (Art. 33 (1) b) ESCB Statute). This particular characteristic has inspired comparisons of the ESCB structure to that of corporations, referring to the ECB as the 'daughter' of the NCBs.[11] Despite the formal economic truth behind this assessment, the comparison is nevertheless substantially misleading, since the provision of financial resources is neither voluntary nor under the control of NCBs (Art. 28 (1), 30 (1) ESCB Statute). More importantly, though, it completely neglects the clear chain of command and position of the ECB within the ESCB.[12] A more accurate depiction of the ESCB structure therefore may be a comparison to other federative entities such as the US Federal Reserve System.[13]

With regard to decision-making, the decentralized approach was abandoned in favour of a centralized top-down governance of the ESCB. This power was conferred to the ECB's governing bodies: The Governing Council and the Executive Board, Art. 282 (2) TFEU, Art. 8, 14 (3) ESCB Statute. A temporary third ECB organ, the General Council (Art. 141 TFEU, Art. 43, 44 ESCB Statute), which will cease to exist once the territorial scope of the Euro area equals that of the EU, is not involved in the decision-making process of the ESCB but rather fulfils coordinating (monetary policies between outs and Euro area) and preparatory (potential Euro area accession) functions (Art. 46 ESCB Statute).[14] A rather new addition to the ECB's internal organisation is the Supervisory Board (Art. 26 SSM Regulation), which conducts the ECB's supervisory tasks under the Single Supervisory Mechanism. Since primary law cannot be overridden by secondary legislation (SSM Regulation), the Supervisory Board formally is no new ECB organ and has to

[8]See https://www.ecb.europa.eu/ecb/orga/capital/html/index.en.html. The amount is adjustable according to a procedure prescribed in Art. 28 (1), 10 (3) ESCB Statute.

[9]The subscription becomes only fully payable upon joining the Euro area. The nine non-Euro area member state NCBs are only required to subscribe financial resources equivalent to the operational costs incurred by the ECB in connection with their participation in the ESCB, https://www.ecb.europa.eu/ecb/orga/capital/html/index.en.html.

[10]Member states and in some cases private shareholders can be considered indirect shareholders of the ECB, as they are shareholders of the NCBs.

[11]Zilioli and Selmayr (2001, p. 72 s).

[12]Smits (1997, p. 94).

[13]Lastra (2015, p. 252 s).

[14]Lastra (2015, p. 251).

submit complete draft decisions to the Governing Council for adoption.[15] Further remarkable features of the ESCB are its status within the EU (only its governing body, the ECB, is an EU institution (Art. 13 TEU). The ESCB is not) and its lack of legal personality (contrary to its components (ECB and NCBs), who do possess legal personality). Only the ECB and NCBs are thus able to sue and be sued.[16] Effectively, this renders the ESCB a collective term for a joint operation of twenty-nine central banks (the ECB and twenty-eight NCBs).[17]

8.1.2 Eurosystem Objectives and Tasks

When carrying out the tasks assigned to them by the treaties the twenty-nine NCBs comprising the ESCB have to act as a whole.[18] Presenting a united front and ensuring the union-wide implementation of centrally agreed measures and policies is paramount for the success of a monetary union. This is why Art. 14 (3) ESCB Statute establishes a clear hierarchy and endows the ECB with authoritative power over the NCBs. The primary objective for the Eurosystem is to pursue price stability within the Euro area. Only in a subsidiary capacity and without prejudice to price stability is it allowed to support the general economic policies of member states (Art. 127 (1) TFEU). Price stability is considered to be one of the main internal factors contributing to monetary stability and is defined by the ECB, in the absence of a legal definition in the treaties, as "a year-on-year increase in the Harmonised Index of Consumer Prices (HICP) for the euro area of below 2%".[19] Historically, the doctrine of price stability goes back to the stability culture of the German Bundesbank and the contemporary economic theory and evidence of the 1980ies/90ies.[20]

In terms of tasks, two categories can be distinguished: There are basic tasks attributed to the Eurosystem in Art. 127 (2) TFEU and other non-basic tasks scattered throughout other provisions, which are usually assigned to the ECB or NCBs specifically. The distinction, however, appears arbitrary and of little practical relevance at times.[21] Of the four basic tasks enumerated in Art. 127 (2) TFEU—(1) to formulate and implement the monetary policy of the Union; (2) to conduct foreign exchange operations; (3) to hold and manage foreign reserve assets and (4) to promote the smooth operation of payments systems—the monetary policy mandate is likely the most significant and in recent years also the most controversial

[15]Lastra (2015, p. 364).

[16]Art. 282 (3) TFEU, Art. 9 (1) and 35 ESCB Statute.

[17]Smits (1997, p. 92 s).

[18]Smits (1997, p. 94).

[19]https://www.ecb.europa.eu/mopo/strategy/pricestab/html/index.en.html.

[20]Lastra (2015, p. 254).

[21]Lastra (2015, p. 255).

one. It is an exclusive competence of the EU (Art. 2 (1), 3 (1) c) TFEU). Logically, the addressees of the monetary policy are only those member states which have already adopted the Euro as currency (see Art. 3 (1) c) TFEU). The conduct of foreign exchange operations is a task the ESCB shares with the Council (Art. 127 (2), 219 TFEU), rendering the external relations of EMU, a rather complex topic. The task generally encompasses the determination of the exchange-rate and regime as well as the management of official foreign reserves.[22] With regard to the holding and management of official foreign reserves, reference may be made to Art. 30 and 31 ESCB Statute, which divide the task between the ECB and NCBs. The NCBs retain a residual competence to hold and manage reserves in order to be able to fulfil the respective member state's commitments towards international organizations (e.g., the IMF, see Chap. 6). In order to promote a smooth operation of payments systems, both the NCBs and ECB are able to offer facilities for cross-union payments systems—usually through the Trans-European Automated Real-time Gross-settlement Express Transfer system (TARGET2)—yet only the ECB possesses regulatory powers to this effect.[23]

Other, as in non-basic, tasks according to Art. 127 (2) TFEU are the issuance of banknotes, Art. 128 (1) TFEU, 16 ESCB Statute (it is unclear why this classic function of central banks is not deemed a basic task in the treaties); the provision of advice to other EU institutions in its field of expertise, Art. 127 (4) TFEU, 4, Art. 34 ESCB Statute; the collection of statistical information, Art. 5 ESCB Statute, and the prudential supervision and stability of the financial system.[24] The latter function was poorly developed at EU level and largely treated as a national matter until recently. Again the financial crisis, which swiftly developed into a sovereign debt crisis in Europe, provided a new impulse for a change of approach towards the issue. The legal option for an expansion of supervisory responsibilities has, however, existed before (Art. 127 (6) TFEU) and was merely taken up by the SSM Regulation.[25]

---

[22]Lastra (2015, p. 264).

[23]TARGET2 is a payment system that settles national and cross-border payments in central bank money and de facto displays the trade balances and capital transfers among Euro area Member States. The incurred cross border transactions normally generate dis-balances, as claims and liabilities at NCBs do not fully balance out. The outstanding claims and liabilities of TARGET2 participating NCBs are then transferred to the ECB and netted out on a daily basis. The cross-border distribution of central bank money within the decentralized structure of the Eurosystem thus continuously causes TARGET2 (net) balances despite the monetary unification. TARGET2 net balances are not functionally equivalent to balance of payments (for as long as the monetary union exists), since they do not lead to an international insolvency of the states consistently running negative balances. For details see Deutsche Bundesbank, Target2 – Balance, https://www.bundesbank.de/Navigation/EN/Tasks/Payment_systems/TARGET2/TARGET2_Balance/target2_balance.html?https=1.

[24]Lastra (2015, p. 266 ss).

[25]For a detailed analysis of the new functions see Lastra (2015, Chap. 10).

8.1.3 ESCB Decision-Making

The decision-making bodies of the ESCB are those of the ECB: The Governing Council and the Executive Board (Art. 282 (2) TFEU). The division of powers between them is outlined in Art. 12 ESCB Statute, which draws a line between the power of making decisions (Governing Council) and the task of ensuring their implementation (Executive Board), thus making the Governing Council the supreme decision-making organ of the ESCB. In their capacity as decision-making organs of the ESCB, they can adopt regulations, take decisions and make recommendations as well as deliver opinions in order to fulfil the tasks endowed to the Eurosystem (the ECB's authority to legislate, Art. 132 (1) TFEU). Additionally, the ECB enjoys the right to be consulted on all legislative drafts dealing with topics which fall within the ECB's realm of competence, both at EU and national level (Art. 282 (5) TFEU). With regard to the content of possible measures, Art. 18–20 ESCB Statute provide a non-exhaustive tool kit, which hands a variety of options to the ECB facilitating adjustable problem-oriented solutions.

The Governing Council consists of the members of the Executive Board (federal element) and the NCB Governors (regional element) of those member states whose currency is the Euro (Art. 10 (1) ESCB Statute). The adoption of decisions follows alternating weighted voting systems—which one applies depends on the respective subject matter at hand (Art. 10 (2) or (3) ESCB Statute)—and can be subject to normal and qualified (two-thirds of the subscribed ECB capital and at least half of the shareholders in favour) majorities.[26] The main difference between both voting systems is that the Executive Board members' votes are not counted when the Governing Council takes decisions relating to Art. 28–29 and 32–33 ESCB Statute. Since those provisions deal with the financial resources of the ECB, which are drawn from the NCBs', disregarding Executive Board members' votes appears to be an appropriate choice. The Governing Council can delegate its powers to the Executive Board where it deems that advisable with the exception of particular tasks specifically assigned to the Council, e.g., Art. 12 (3), 35 (5), 14 (2), 41 ESCB Statute.[27]

The Executive Board on the other hand consists of the ECB President and Vice-President as well as four other members, who are appointed by the European Council for non-renewable eight year terms (Art. 11 (2) ESCB Statute). The Board's function is mainly a managerial one, implementing the monetary policy set by the Governing Council, instructing NCBs accordingly, preparing the meetings of the Governing Council and managing the ECB (Art. 11 (6), 12 (1), (2) ESCB Statute). The Executive Board is based on the 'one man one vote' principle and in the event of a tie the ECB President has the casting vote, as he does in the Governing Council.[28]

[26]Smits (1997, p. 99 ss).

[27]Smits (1997, p. 96).

[28]Smits (1997, p. 101 ss).

The work of both decision-making bodies is prepared and supported by the ESCB staff, which is organized in special committees and often further subdivided in working groups or task forces.[29] In contrast to the absence of judicial review options in the IMF legal framework, it has been clear ever since the OLAF decision of the ECJ[30] that the ECB is subject to judicial review and that the shield of independence (see below) does not extend further than its express powers.[31] This conclusion can, however, also be drawn based on Art. 35 (1) ESCB Statute alone. Note that claims against the ECB or NCBs are not claims against the ESCB (which lacks legal personality), nor against the EU or the respective member state.

8.1.4 Central Bank Independence

A key feature, if not the defining one, of the ECB is the principle of central bank independence (Art. 130 TFEU).[32] For the NCBs, central bank independence is a criterion of legal convergence, a condition for the ability to join the Euro area (Art. 131 TFEU). The principle of independence shields the ECB and NCBs from any form of exercised influence when performing their treaty functions by safeguarding the ECB's functional, organizational and financial independence.[33] Furthermore, it ensures their decisions to be guided by the objectives set out in Art. 127 TFEU and nothing else. As a matter of fact, price stability is one of the main rationales behind the establishment of independent central banks. Past experiences have shown that the pursuit of inflationary policies often is an attractive solution for other political institutions, specifically governments, since they offer immediate short-term relief to economic and fiscal issues, which are cumbersome (and often unpopular with voters) to overcome otherwise.[34]

8.2 ECOFIN Council and Eurogroup

The Economic and Financial Affairs Council (ECOFIN Council) is the Council (Art. 16 TEU) in its composition of economic and finance ministers. Generally responsible for economic policy and taxation matters as well as the regulation of financial services, it has some functions which have important implications for the monetary union. Among these are the coordination of economic policies and in

[29] ECB (2011, p. 21).

[30] ECJ, OLAF, C-11/00, p. 135.

[31] Lastra (2015, p. 272).

[32] See Lastra (2015, p. 269 ss).

[33] Lastra (2015, p. 270).

[34] Lastra (2015, p. 67 ss).

particular the surveillance of budgetary discipline (Art. 120, 121, 136, 137 TFEU), a decisive role in the Euro area enlargement procedure (Art. 139, 140 TFEU) and the right to adopt special measures in times of crisis (Art. 122, 143, 144 TFEU). Note, however, that Art. 139 (4) in conjunction with (2) TFEU suspends the voting rights of council members, representing non-Euro area Member States, for matters concerning core interests of the Euro area.

The Eurogroup is an informal body, now mentioned in Art. 137 TFEU and further regulated in Protocol No 14, which represents a forum for the ministers of Euro area member states to discuss matters related to the Euro and to coordinate their actions. Usually, the Eurogroup prepares ECOFIN Council meetings by coordinating Members States' positions prior to these meetings. No binding decisions can be adopted in the Eurogroup due to its informal role. Yet the deepened coordination unfolds its effect once the ECOFIN Council decides on the respective issues as only Euro area Member States are allowed to vote on matters concerning core interests of the Euro area.

The Euro Summit is the counterpart of the Eurogroup on heads of state or government level and was created during the crisis to provide further strategic guidance on euro area economic policy. It consists of the heads of state or government of the euro area countries, the Euro Summit President and the President of the European Commission and is supposed to meet at least twice a year (Art. 12 Treaty on Stability, Coordination and Governance in the EMU, TSCG).

8.3 Commission

The Commission plays a rather supporting role in EMU and generally offers advice through recommendations and proposals (see Art. 135, 144 (2) TFEU). It holds a more significant role in the realm of economic policy coordination and budgetary discipline supervision though (Art. 121 and 126 TFEU), as the Commission is tasked with surveillance and controlling functions there.

8.4 Economic and Financial Committee

The Economic and Financial Committee is the successor of the Monetary Committee and has mostly advisory and supporting functions (Art. 134 TFEU). The Committee comprises six members, whereof the Commission, the ECB and the member states each appoint two.

References

ECB (2011) The Monetary policy of the ECB 2011. https://www.ecb.europa.eu/pub/pdf/other/monetarypolicy2011en.pdf

Lastra R (2015) International financial and monetary law, 2nd edn. Oxford University Press, Oxford

Moutot P, Jung A, Mongelli P (2008) The workings of the Eurosystem, ECB Occasional Paper Series No 79 2008. ECB, Frankfurt am Main. https://www.ecb.europa.eu/pub/pdf/scpops/ecbocp79.pdf?66c7d93f692dd780314145ae6772f03d

Smits R (1997) The European Central Bank, institutional aspects, 1st edn. Kluwer Law International, The Hague

Zilioli C, Selmayr M (2001) The Law of the European Central Bank, 1st edn. Hart Publishing, Oxford

Chapter 9
The Substantive Legal Foundations of EMU post Lisbon

EMU serves important objectives of the EU, e.g. the smooth operation of the internal market, coordination of economic and fiscal policies, price stability and supervising and monitoring financial institutions, which have long left the confinement of national borders.[1] To this end, EMU displays certain key characteristics, which have a significant impact on the economic life within the union but also in relation to third countries and non-Euro area members.

9.1 Basic Features of EMU

A currency union is defined by and requires certain elements in order to replace the individual currencies of its members with a new 'single currency' and organize the exercise of monetary sovereignty jointly. EMU is the prime example of such a currency union in the world and it goes well beyond merely introducing the Euro as the currency of the EU. The legal framework does provide for a Euro area wide central banking system, for free movement of payments and capital as well as payment systems, for monetary and exchange-rate policy making and—last but not least—for budgetary and economic policy coordination.

9.2 Membership and Territorial Scope of the Euro Area: Ins and Outs

Participation in the Euro area and thus the adoption of the Euro is formulated as a general obligation of all EU Member States in the treaties, see Art. 3 (4) TEU, 119 (2) TFEU. Yet membership of the Euro area is subject to specific conditions whose

[1]European Commission, How economic and monetary union works, http://ec.europa.eu/economy_finance/euro/emu/how/index_en.htm.

C. Herrmann and C. Dornacher, *International and European Monetary Law*, SpringerBriefs in Law, DOI 10.1007/978-3-319-57642-8_9

rationale reflects the need for a minimum of economic homogeneity among the participants of the single currency. Otherwise, the centrifugal forces will become too strong to hold the union together.[2] Due to the special status of two Member States (UK, Denmark) and other Member States not fulfilling the required conditions yet, the Euro area became the first comprehensive project of differentiated integration within the EU.[3] Three categories of Member States can thus be distinguished: (1) Euro area Member States ("ins"); (2) Member States with a derogation in stage three of EMU (non-compliance with all convergence criteria) ("pre-ins") and (3) Member States with a special status ("outs").[4]

9.2.1 Convergence Criteria

The conditions that govern the accession to the Euro area are called convergence criteria (see Art, 140 (1) TFEU). Further details are provided in the Protocols No. 13 (convergence criteria) and No. 12 (excessive deficit procedure). The criteria are commonly referred to as the "Maastricht Criteria":[5]

- *Compatibility of national legislation with EU treaties and the ESCB Statute*
  The legal convergence criterion, often overlooked in discussions on the Maastricht Criteria, ensures that NCBs are independent and ready to operate in the ESCB structure from a regulatory perspective.[6]
- *Achieving a high degree of price stability*
  Due to the primary commitment of the ESCB to price stability (Art. 127 (1) TFEU), becoming an integral part of that system requires a low-inflationary environment. Whether a prospective Member State achieves a high degree of price stability is benchmarked against the average inflation rates of the three best performing Member States in that regard (Art. 140 (1) TFEU, Art. 1 Protocol No. 13).[7] The prospective Member State's price performance should be sustainable and its average rate of inflation should not exceed 1.5% points above that of the reference rate of the three least inflationary Member States within the past year (Art. 1 Protocol No. 13).
- *Sustainable government budgetary position*
  The convergence criterion of sustainable government finances is defined as the absence of excessive budgetary deficits (Art. 140 (1) TFEU, Art. 2 Protocol

[2]Proctor (1999, p. 53).

[3]Zilioli and Selmayr (2001, p. 133).

[4]See Zilioli and Selmayr (2001, p. 134 ss).

[5]See Smits (1997, p. 121).

[6]Smits (1997, p. 121 s).

[7]In the event of a significant gap between the two best performing Member States to the third best, only the first two serve as reference point. This follows from the formulation "at most" in Art. 1 Protocol No. 13, see Smits (1997, p. 123).

No. 13). Pursuant to Art. 2 Protocol No. 13, this criterion is met if, at the time of the assessment, no Council decision according to Art. 126 (6) (2), Art. 1 Protocol No. 12 exists, asserting the excessiveness of the budgetary deficit.

- *Normal fluctuation margins of exchange-rates*
  Furthermore, prospective Euro area Member States are required to observe the normal margins of exchange-rate fluctuation within ERM II against the Euro without severe tensions in at least the past two years prior to the assessment (Art. 140 (1) TFEU, Art. 3 Protocol No. 13). In particular, the respective Member State would be ineligible for membership if it devaluated its currency deliberately against the Euro within the relevant assessment period (Art. 3 Protocol No. 13). Normal margins of fluctuation are ±15% above or below the central rate.[8]
- *Durability of Convergence*
  Finally, prospective Member States need to prove their capability of durable convergence between themselves and the Euro area Member States' economies and currency. To this end, long-term interest rates on long-term government bonds and comparable securities should not exceed those of the, at most, three best performing Member States in terms of price stability by more than 2% (Art. 140 (1) TFEU, Art. 4 Protocol No. 13). This essentially leads to a market test of confidence in the currency and finances of the respective Member States. Together with the prohibition of excessive deficits, it illustrates the regulatory approach of EMU quite well: A system based on prevention and conditioning by market forces (see also Art. 123–125 TFEU).

The convergence criteria are amendable by unanimous decision of the ECOFIN Council pursuant to a proposal by the Commission and after consulting with the European Parliament, the ECB and the Economic and Financial Committee (Art. 6 Protocol No. 13). The unanimity requirement played a decisive role in the Maastricht judgment of the German Constitutional Court since it prevents any alteration of the admittance criteria for new Euro area members without prior consent of all Member States.[9]

9.2.2 Procedure

Member states with a derogation, i.e. members that are not yet eligible for Euro area membership (Art. 139 (1) TFEU; so-called pre-ins), nevertheless participate in stage three of EMU and are obliged to make efforts towards achieving the necessary convergence. Their progress is regularly monitored by the Commission and the ECB, who submit convergence reports at least every two years or upon request by a

---

[8]European Commission, What is ERM II? http://ec.europa.eu/economy_finance/euro/adoption/erm2/index_en.htm.

[9]BVerfG, Maastricht judgement, BVerfGE 89, 155, para. 144.

prospective Member State (Art. 140 (1) TFEU). The formal decision on enlarging the Euro area is a prerogative of the Council, which abrogates the derogation status of the respective Member State following a proposal by the Commission and after consulting with the European Parliament and a discussion of the matter in the European Council. The Council decides according to a recommendation of the Euro Group, adopted by a qualified majority, (Art. 140 (2) TFEU). The irrevocable fix of the exchange-rate between the respective Member State's national currency and the Euro, which is also the base for the conversion/replacement of the former, is set by the Council. Again, the decision is taken pursuant to a proposal by the Commission, after consulting the ECB and in accordance with a unanimous recommendation of the Euro Group and the respective Member State (Art. 140 (3) TFEU).

9.2.3 The Exception: "Outs"

Two EU Member States are exempted from participation in the Euro area irrespective of their level of convergence: The UK and Denmark. Rather than being subject to the admission automatism outlined above, they will only ever have to introduce the Euro and comply with all provisions of EMU if they positively opt to do so. The UK and Denmark were granted their special status in two separate Protocols, No. 15 (UK) and 16 (Denmark), giving them the right to choose whether or not to proceed to stage three of EMU and join the Euro area.[10] Albeit enjoying an effectively similar status,[11] their positions differ legally. The UK on the one hand has opted out of participating in stage three of EMU altogether and is exempt from pursuing the single currency objective. In addition, the independence requirement does not apply to the Bank of England and the UK has only limited obligations to comply with governmental budgetary discipline (Art. 3–10 Protocol No. 15). Denmark on the other hand is treated as a state with a derogation (Art. 1 Protocol No. 16, see Art. 139 TFEU) pursuant to availing itself of its exemption option by unilateral declaration.[12] The difference to other states with a derogation results from the reason for the derogation status. Normally, Member States have a derogation because they failed the convergence criteria test. Their derogation is only temporary. Denmark on the other hand has a derogation due to voluntary withdrawal from the automatism process and is only treated as a derogation state because Protocol 16 declares the derogation provisions applicable to Denmark.[13] The UK Protocol uses a different legal technique and enumerates all provisions which are applicable to the UK despite its non-participation in stage three of EMU.[14] However, the difference

[10]Zilioli and Selmayr (2001, p. 137).

[11]Zilioli and Selmayr (2001, p. 142).

[12]Denmark notified the Council accordingly on November 3, 1993, see Art. 1 Protocol No. 16.

[13]Smits (1997, p. 137 s).

[14]For a detailed study of the status of the UK and Denmark see Zilioli and Selmayr (2001, p. 137 ss).

is very small in practice. Finally, there is also the de facto option of gaining a semi-permanent derogation status by deliberate non-compliance with all or parts of the convergence criteria and thus remaining in an "endless" Art. 140 (1) TFEU procedure loop. Sweden devised this strategy after a negative referendum from its people regarding the adoption of the Euro.[15]

9.2.4 Relationship Between Ins and Outs

The resulting differentiated integration has institutional and substantial legal effects in terms of applicable provisions and participation in decision-making bodies. A special regime applies to the "pre-ins and outs", which generally includes all economic provisions, except for the excessive deficit sanctions (Art. 126 (9) and (11) TFEU), but limits monetary provisions to those applicable during stage two.[16]

The status of Member States with a derogation is regulated in Art. 139 TFEU. Art. 139 (2) TFEU enumerates provisions where 'Member State' is to be read as Euro area Member State, thus stripping the "pre-ins" and Denmark of a number of rights (e.g. voting rights (Art. 139 (2), (4)), appointment of the Executive Board, monetary income of the ESCB) and obligations (e.g. legal acts of the ECB, objectives and tasks of the ESCB, issuance of the Euro, subscription to the capital of the ECB). The rights and obligations of the UK are regulated in Protocol No. 15. With regard to the institutional set-up, all "outs" (pre-ins plus Denmark and the UK) are represented and present at Council meetings concerning Euro area issues, but are not allowed to vote. Conversely, they are not even represented in the decision-making bodies of the ESCB (Governing Council, Executive Board), but are only part of the largely advisory body, the General Council.[17] The exchange-rate—the most tangible relation between the Euro and the currencies of all "outs"—can be regulated by the ERM II and subject to fixed but adjustable rates.

9.2.5 Termination of Membership

During the height of the "Greek crisis" the dictum "Grexit" began to widely circulate and stir controversy. The neologism is a common name for various ideas dealing with the voluntary or compulsory Euro area exit of a Member State (in this case Greece) while still remaining in the EU. These kind of considerations are not

[15]European Commission, Eurobarometer—Post-referendum in Sweden, http://ec.europa.eu/public_opinion/flash/fl149_en.pdf.

[16]Smits (1997, p. 135).

[17]Zilioli and Selmayr (2001), provide a detailed analysis of the special regime applying to the "outs", p. 144 ss.

new,[18] yet the subject matter swiftly gained in significance and urgency after Greece's continued fiscal struggles. As a matter of fact, the treaties do contain a provision for leaving the EU altogether (Art. 50 TEU), but no such regulation exists for the Euro area. Nonetheless, by means of an "a maiore ad minus" argument, the exit from a subset of the EU may be conceivable. Yet, with regard to the purpose of EMU and specifically the single currency as well as the irreversibility of the Euro,[19] the majority read of EU law is that it is legally not possible to terminate the Euro area membership, either unilaterally or by multilateral agreement or expulsion, without at the same time ending that state's membership of the European Union as a whole.[20] Note that the use of the ordinary revision procedure (Art. 48 TEU) remains a possible option to amend EU law accordingly, since the Member States are the "masters of the treaties".[21]

9.3 The Euro as Legal Tender

Upon entry into the third stage of EMU on January 1st 1999, the Euro became a currency in its own right, fulfilling the objective set out in Art. 3 (4) TEU.[22] Most importantly, a detailed legal framework was required to facilitate the substitution of national currencies and address all practical issues arising from a change of currency. The treaties offer only cornerstones, whereas the main source for the Euro framework is now contained in several secondary law acts based on Art. 352 and 114 TFEU. The legislative competence is provided for in Art. 133 TFEU.

9.3.1 *Legal Tender Status and Issuance of Banknotes and Coins*

Art. 128 (1) TFEU in conjunction with Art. 10 and 11 of Regulation (EC) 974/1998 awards the Euro banknotes and coins the status of sole legal tender in the Euro area. The physical issuance of said banknotes is the task of the ECB and the NCBs according to an allocation key and subject to the authorization by the Governing Council of the ECB (Art. 128 TFEU, Art. 16 ESCB Statute).[23]

[18] See for example, Proctor (1999, p. 225 ss).

[19] See Proctor (1999, p. 226).

[20] Herrmann (2015), Athanassiou (2009, p. 27 ss and p. 36), Wieduwilt (2015, p. 192 s). Note that the existence of an exit clause would pose great speculative threats for the Euro.

[21] Herrmann (2002, p. 4), Proctor (1999, p. 227), Wieduwilt (2015, p. 193).

[22] Proctor (1999, p. 21).

[23] Lastra (2015, p. 275). The issuance of coins is a right of the Member States' Governments, subject to ECB authorization.

9.3.2 Regulations Introducing the Euro

Before a new currency can enter the stage, however, the legacy of the old ones needs to be dealt with. Therefore, Regulation (EC) No 1103/97, based on Art. 352 TFEU and applicable in all EU Member States, provides for the continuity of contracts and resolves issues related to ECU-denominated obligations as well as issues of conversion and rounding.[24] The initial participating Member States were listed in the Council Decision (EC) 317/98.[25] The list defined the territorial scope of Regulation (EC) 974/98,[26] which gradually introduced the euro banknotes and coins over a transitional period and regulated the sequenced full substitution of national currencies. For the purposes of the transitional period, national currency units were declared sub-divisions of the Euro, to the effect that for the duration of this phase national currency units and Euro units were units of the same currency.[27] The legal tender status of national currency banknotes and coins ceased six months after the end of the transitional period at the latest. Nonetheless, NCBs still continue to convert banknotes and coins previously issued by them into Euro at the conversion rate determined by Council Regulation (EC) 2866/98.[28]

More technical issues are covered in the Council Regulation (EC) 975/98 on denomination and technical specifications of Euro coins and in the ECB Decision (ECB/2003/4), which regulates the protection from reproduction, the exchange of damaged or mutilated banknotes and withdrawal of banknotes.[29] With regard to protecting the Euro, a mention of the Council Regulation (EC) 1338/2001 needs to be made. Said Regulation is concerned with fighting counterfeiting and falsification of Euro banknotes and coins, an issue which was initially left to the Member States (Art. 12 Regulation (EC) No. 974/1998) but subsequently centralized. The ECB even established a Counterfeit Analysis Centre (CAC) in Frankfurt.

9.3.3 The Euro in Third Countries

Due to historic and/or geographic reasons, several Euro area Member States had special monetary relations with certain entities prior to the introduction of the

---

[24]Lastra (2015, p. 276); for a detailed study of the legal effects of the Euro introduction see Proctor (1999, p. 107 ss).

[25]Proctor (1999, p. 21).

[26]The regulation is based on Art. 140 (3) TFEU.

[27]Lastra (2015, p. 277).

[28]See for example Deutsche Bundesbank, DM banknotes and coins, https://www.bundesbank.de/Navigation/EN/Tasks/Cash_management/DM_banknotes_and_coins/dm.html?nsc=true&https=1; ECB, Evaluation of the 2002 cash changeover, https://www.ecb.europa.eu/pub/pdf/other/cashchangeoverreport2002en.pdf.

[29]Lastra (2015, pp. 279, 282).

Euro.[30] This concerns states and territories like the Vatican City, San Marino, Andorra and Monaco, which were using Member States' currencies as legal tender before. For the lack of EU jurisdiction over these states and territories, the abovementioned Regulations are not automatically applicable there. The matter was resolved in different ways but often by new monetary agreements entitling the respective entities to use the Euro as official currency and legal tender.[31] Some states even began to use the Euro as legal tender without the explicit authorization by the ECB or the ESCB (e.g. Montenegro and Kosovo).[32]

9.4 Free Movement of Capital and Payments

9.4.1 Reasons for the Liberalization

Historically, the evolution of EMU was linked to the completion of the internal market and is testimony to integration generating the need for further integration. A necessary equivalent of the liberalization of goods and service flows therefore was and is the liberalization of capital and payments flows.[33] While being vital components of the internal market both capital and payments mobility are also prerequisites for completing the monetary union. A single monetary policy requires a single monetary zone as a reference point.[34] Due to the non-existence of a European State, whose territory would automatically produce a single monetary zone, those particular barriers had to be torn down first using legal provisions.

9.4.2 Content and Scope of the Freedom

9.4.2.1 General Freedom

The free movement of capital and payments is one of the fundamental freedoms guaranteed within the EU and enjoys direct effect in all Member States, i.e. is directly enforceable in Member States' courts and takes precedence over any contradictory national law.[35] Unlike other fundamental freedoms, it is not limited to the territory of

[30]Lastra (2015, p. 282).

[31]Lastra (2015, p. 282 ss).

[32]Lastra (2015, p. 283 s).

[33]Smits (1997, p. 57).

[34]Proctor (1999, p. 80).

[35]ECJ, Sanz de Lera, C-250/94, para. 40 ss; the prerequisites for direct effect are: Clear and unambiguous wording as well as no need for further intermediary national acts in order to implement the provision.

the EU but instead includes monetary flows to third countries as well. This particular liberalization therefor applies erga omnes (Art. 63 (1) TFEU).[36] As far as payments are concerned this is hardly a regulatory novelty, since it correlates with the Member States' obligations under the (nearly globally binding) IMF Articles of Agreement. In terms of capital mobility, the fundamental freedom does, of course, extend beyond the IMF obligations of the Member States.[37]

9.4.2.2 Exceptions

The liberalization is not absolute but rather subject to specific exceptions and qualifications in content. These are:

- Justifications for restrictions of the free movement of capital with third countries (Art. 64 and 66 TFEU);
- justifications for restrictions of both capital and payments mobility with third countries (Art. 75 TFEU);
- justifications for overriding reasons of general public interest (Cassis de Dijon case law);
- qualification of certain measures as non-restrictive with regard to both capital and payments mobility (Art. 65 (1) a) TFEU) and justifications for restrictions of both freedoms (Art. 65 (1) b) TFEU);
- "escape clauses", which permit even intra-EU restrictions of capital and payments transfers in case of severe balance-of-payments problems (Art. 143 and 144 TFEU).[38]

The latter can only be invoked by Member States with a derogation. The differentiation between "ins" and "outs" in that regard stems from the fact that there are no longer any balance-of-payments between Euro area Members which could justify the restrictions. The fate of pre-existing, i.e. before the establishment of EMU, national and European restrictions of capital flows to and from third countries is dealt with in Art. 64 TFEU, which basically constitutes a standstill-clause. The reference date is December 31, 1993 and it involves measures adopted in four areas: Direct investment; establishment; financial services and admission of securities to capital markets. The pre-existing restrictions can be varied or even revoked through the ordinary legislative procedure by the European Parliament together with the Council (Art. 64 (2), 294 TFEU). New measures in these areas can be adopted unanimously by the Council through the special legislative procedure (Art. 64 (3) TFEU). Another EU competence for capital movement restrictions is

[36]Smits (1997, p. 59).

[37]Generally on freedom of capital movements and payments see Commission, Staff working document on the movement of capital, http://ec.europa.eu/finance/capital/docs/reports/2015-market-monitoring-working-document_en.pdf.

[38]Smits (1997, p. 60).

contained in Art. 66 TFEU. Measures adopted pursuant to this provision are not limited to specific areas of capital flows, but may only be applied in emergency situations, e.g. if the movement of capital undermines the monetary policy of the ECB or the operation of the EMU as a whole.[39] Besides such monetary emergency incidents, restrictions can also be implemented due to political emergencies, more precisely to counter terrorism, by freezing assets and accounts (Art. 75 TFEU). The Council is competent to adopt such measures in accordance with a regulation of the European Parliament and the Council.[40] However, following the ECJ Cassis de Dijon case law Member States retain their competence to introduce restrictions due to overriding reasons of general public interest. Any measures adopted under this "unwritten" justification must be non-discriminatory, as well as suitable and proportionate in light of the objective.[41] Recent examples for Member States availing themselves of this possibility are Cyprus[42] and Greece.[43] Finally, Art. 65 TFEU ascertains that tax regulations do not qualify as restrictions of either freedom. In addition to that, the provision also contains justifications for measures of Member States which restrict financial flows (e.g. security and safety reasons).

References

Athanassiou P (2009) Withdrawal and expulsion from EU and EMU, ECB legal working paper series No. 10/December 2009. ECB, Frankfurt am Main

Herrmann C (2002) Monetary sovereignty over the Euro and the external relations of the Euro area: Competences, procedures and practice. Eur Foreign Aff Rev 7(1):1–24

Herrmann C (2015) Searching for the Ariadne's thread—the legal complexities of "Grexit" and "Graccident". Verfassungsblog. http://verfassungsblog.de/auf-der-suche-nach-dem-ariadnefaden-von-den-rechtlichen-schwierigkeiten-von-grexit-und-graccident-2/

Lastra R (2015) International financial and monetary law, 2nd edn. Oxford University Press, Oxford

Proctor C (1999) The Euro and the financial markets, 1st edn. Jordan Publishing Limited, Bristol

Smits R (1997) The European Central Bank, institutional aspects. Kluwer Law International, The Hague

Wieduwilt S (2015) Article 50 TEU—the legal framework of a withdrawal from the European Union. ZEuS 18(2):169–205

Zilioli C, Selmayr M (2001) The Law of the European Central Bank. Hart Publishing, Oxford

---

[39]Smits (1997, p. 62).

[40]See in this context the communication, COM (2016) 50, of the Commission on an action plan for strengthening the fight against terrorist financing, p. 10 ss, http://ec.europa.eu/transparency/regdoc/rep/1/2016/EN/1-2016-50-EN-1-1.PDF.

[41]ECJ, Cassis de Dijon, C-120/78, para. 8.

[42]Commission, Staff working document on the movement of capital, p. 25 s, http://ec.europa.eu/finance/capital/docs/reports/2015-market-monitoring-working-document_en.pdf.
and the freedom of payments.

[43]See Commission, Statement on the capital controls imposed by the Greek authorities, http://europa.eu/rapid/press-release_STATEMENT-15-5271_en.htm?locale=en.

Chapter 10
The Monetary Policy of EMU

10.1 Legal Foundations and Limits

The ability to set the monetary policy and regulate one's own currency is a classical attribute of state sovereignty. By transferring these powers to the EU, where they are exercised by the Eurosystem (Art. 127 (2), 282 (1) TFEU), the Council and the Parliament (Art. 133 TFEU), the Euro area Member States have effectively transferred their monetary sovereignty to the supranational EU.[1]

10.1.1 What is Monetary Policy and How Does it Work?

Monetary policy is the sum of all actions taken by monetary authorities to control the supply and cost (interest rates) of money and credit within a specific monetary area.[2] The majority of today's existing central bank statutes, however, do not include a definition of monetary policy. It is instead common legislative practice to endow the task to a specific institution (e.g. a central bank), which is tasked to pursue one or more objectives with the instruments provided for in the statutes,[3] (the ESCB Statute is no exception). Yet, monetary policy is not necessarily formulated and implemented by the same authority. Independent central banks, for example, formulate as well as implement monetary policies, whereas dependent central banks are usually restricted to implementing policies formulated by governments.[4] Bound by specific goals (e.g. Art. 127 (1) TFEU) most independent

[1]The issue of who is the holder of the monetary sovereignty (EU, ECB, ESCB or the Euro area Member States conjointly) has been the subject of vigorous debate among academics: See Lastra (2015, p. 22), Herrmann (2010, p. 118 ss), Zilioli and Selmayr (2001, p. 13 ss).
[2]Lastra (2015, p. 37), Proctor (1999, p. 74).
[3]Lastra (2015, p. 37).
[4]Lastra (2015, p. 38).

C. Herrmann and C. Dornacher, *International and European Monetary Law*,
SpringerBriefs in Law, DOI 10.1007/978-3-319-57642-8_10

central banks, however, do not enjoy "absolute independence".[5] They are typically endowed with discretionary powers regarding the strategy and choice of instruments ("operational independence") though, as these decisions require economic rather than legal or political expertise.[6] Admittedly, the long-term distributional effects of monetary policies, e.g. very low interest rates favouring debtors over savers or trusts, are another issue, which is not (and probably cannot be) properly addressed by central bank laws.[7] Within the EMU legal framework considerations of this kind may be effected via the principle of proportionality (Art. 5 (4) TEU).[8]

In practice, monetary policy cannot directly influence the objectives set out in the statutes (e.g. price stability, Art. 127 (1) TFEU), since neither governments nor central banks control prices, production or employment developments etc. in free market economies. The available monetary instruments are therefor used to alter specific targets, like the monetary base or the central interest rate, which in turn affect the behaviour or expectations of market participants and are up to a certain degree capable of managing the demand and supply of money. The ultimate objectives (in the case of EMU primarily price stability, Art. 127 (1) TFEU) can thus solely be achieved via various so-called 'monetary transmission channels'.[9] Transmission channels are the causal "links through which monetary policy impulses are transferred to the real economy".[10] Market participants (commercial banks, investors etc.) function as intermediates, who act or react upon the monetary authority's (in the case of EMU: the Eurosystem's) use of monetary instruments.

There are five main monetary transmission channels: (1) the interest rate channel depicts the transmission of central bank interest rates for commercial banks to private consumers and businesses; (2) the credit channel illustrates the changing lending activity of commercial banks (quantity of loans) due to fluctuations of interest rates[11]; (3) closely linked to both is the risk-taking channel, which shows adaptions in the risk affinity of market participants. Very low interest rates for example make riskier deals more attractive as they may still offer good yields; (4) the exchange-rate channel affects policy objectives by changes in domestic prices for imported goods and impacts on the domestic competitiveness in international markets; (5) finally the expectation channel, which relies on the credibility of central bank communication and describes the attempt of influencing private sector long-term expectations.[12] The entire process of transmitting monetary policy

[5]Lastra (2015, p. 38).

[6]Lastra (2015, p. 40 s).

[7]Lastra (2015, p. 43).

[8]Generally for the application of the proportionality test see the opinion of Advocate General C. Villalón in the Gauweiler case (C-62/14), para. 159 ss.

[9]ECB (2011, p. 58 ss).

[10]ECB (2011, p. 59).

[11]ECB (2011, p. 60).

[12]ECB (2011, p. 61); An example of this may be the press release announcing the OMT Program, which was subsequently never implemented because its mere announcement sufficed to provoke the desired market reactions.

to the real economy is highly complex and while the basic principle is widely accepted and understood there is no consensus among experts on the details of the mechanism's functioning.

Consequently, the monetary policy of independent central banks is usually based on a vast supply of diverse economic information and developments and ideally guided only by the legally prescribed objectives. The ECB for example devised a "two-pillar" analysis strategy based on economic and monetary trends.[13]

10.1.2 The Eurosystem's Monetary Policy Mandate

The parameters of the legal mandate of the Eurosystem with regard to monetary policy are contained in Art. 127 (1) and (2) TFEU, 282 (1) and (2) TFEU, Art. 2 and 3.1 ESCB Statute. These provisions clearly confer the competence to define and implement the monetary policy for the Euro area to the Eurosystem. The monetary policy mandate constitutes an exclusive competence, i.e. only the respective bodies of the EU can adopt legally valid acts in these areas (Art. 2 (1), 3 (1) c) TFEU). Note that the exclusive right is strictly confined to the scope of the conferred power as specified in the treaties (principle of conferral, Art. 5 (2) TEU) and any extension beyond that would constitute an infringement of the Member States' competences and thus be invalid. The precise determination of the mandate's scope, however, is significantly impeded by the lack of a legal definition of monetary policy in the treaties. The matter is further complicated by the close proximity and interplay of economic policies—mainly a Member State competence (but see Art. 5 (1) TFEU)[14]—and monetary policies in reality.

Opinions on how to define monetary policy were divided before and during the euro sovereign debt crisis with some voicing that the Eurosystem is restricted to a seemingly enumerated set of instruments and that the effects of the instrument used would largely determine the nature of the measure.[15] Others acknowledged that both economic and monetary policy decisions influence each other and regularly show cross-policy effects, sometimes even need to do so in order to accomplish the objectives set out in the treaties (see the transmission channels of monetary policy above).[16] Hence, the effect of a policy is ill-suited to determine the nature of said policy. Furthermore, the treaties do not contain an exhaustive enumeration of possible instruments but rather explicitly provide the option to create new instruments whenever the Eurosystem deems it necessary in the light of the objectives

[13]ECB (2011, p. 83).

[14]Notwithstanding the primacy of price stability, the Eurosystem shall support the general economic policies in the EU though, Art. 127 (1) TFEU.

[15]Murswiek (2014, p. 151); similarly BVerfG, reference for a preliminary ruling in Gauweiler, 2 BvR 2728/13, para. 65.

[16]Thiele (2014, p. 259).

mentioned in Art. 127 TFEU (see Art. 20 ESCB Statute).[17] Ultimately, the question was referred twice to the ECJ,[18] which established some basic rules regarding the interpretation of the Eurosystem's mandate. First of all, the court held in *Pringle* that cross-policy effects or indirect contributions to the objectives allotted to competences of Member States in the treaties is itself not sufficient to alter the nature of the measure.[19] Secondly, it was clarified once more in *Gauweiler* that the assessment of a measure's nature principally depends on the objective pursued by said measure (as stipulated by the acting body). Additionally, the employed instruments may also be relevant.[20]

In conclusion, monetary policy is therefore mainly defined by the objectives pursued with a measure and in a subordinate capacity by the instruments used—a seemingly vague and broad definition of a competence. Nevertheless, the contours of the mandate are much sharper than it may seem. Art. 127 (1) TFEU clearly enumerates and ranks the objectives monetary policy can validly pursue under EU law (primacy of price stability). Moreover, the provision obliges the Eurosystem to respect the principles laid out in Art. 3 TEU and 119 TFEU; among them are the principles of sound public finances and of free market economies as well as the efficient allocation of resources. These obligations limit the scale of latitude for the Eurosystem significantly and also prevent it from undermining the economic or fiscal policies of Member States.

Concerning the objectives of the Eurosystem, the primacy of price stability is defined by the ECB as "a year-on-year increase in the Harmonised Index of Consumer Prices (HICP) for the euro area of below (but close to) 2%".[21] This particular choice of target reflects specific economic considerations but does not represent the only legally possible or valid interpretation of price stability. Indeed, some commentators even regard a slightly higher target rate to be still compatible with the meaning of Art. 127 (1) TFEU.[22] In practice, the—for EU law rather unique—hierarchy of objectives (e.g. see Art. 3 TEU, which does not rank objectives)[23] means that the preservation of price stability will always prevail over the achievement of any other goal in case of conflict irrespective of how legitimate or politically desirable the other objective may be at the time. The precise content of the subordinate objective "support the general economic policies in the Union" on the other hand remains somewhat unclear. The only firm conclusion that can be drawn from Art. 127 (1) TFEU read in conjunction with Art. 130 TFEU (central bank independence) is that it is up to the Eurosystem to substantiate it in practice. Furthermore, it follows from the general understanding of the term "support" that

[17]See also Smits (1997, pp. 283–288).

[18]Pringle, C-370/12 and Gauweiler, C-62/14.

[19]ECJ, Pringle, C-370/12, para. 56 and 96 s.

[20]ECJ, Gauweiler, C-62/14, para. 46 ss; see already ECJ, Pringle, C-370/12, para. 53, 55 and 56 s.

[21]See https://www.ecb.europa.eu/stats/macroeconomic_and_sectoral/hicp/html/index.en.html.

[22]Thiele (2015, p. 296); see also Selmayr (2015, § 23, para. 98).

[23]Selmayr (2015, § 23, para. 89).

the Eurosystem cannot take on a leading role in European economic policies.[24] It may be another matter if the Member States were to delegate certain substantial economic policy tasks to the Eurosystem, since the exercise of delegated powers could be viewed as exercising a supporting role rather than a leading one. However, the legal assessment of such a delegation would largely depend on the specific circumstances. Anyhow, a delegation of this kind would need to fully respect the principle of independence as well as be in line with the objective of price stability.

Despite the positive obligation to pursue price stability, the treaties also prohibit certain actions known to be prone to inflation or undermining the independence of the ECB. Accordingly, Art. 123 (1) TFEU (and Art. 21 ESCB-Statute) prohibits the ECB and NCBs to offer overdraft or any other credit facilities to Member States or any EU institution/body/agency as well as to purchase bonds *directly* from them on primary markets (so called "prohibition of monetary state financing"). Publicly owned credit institutions (e.g. Sparkassen) are specifically excluded from the scope of the prohibition (Art. 123 (2) TFEU). They are to be treated like private credit institutions by the ECB and NCBs.[25] The prohibition is a substantive limitation of central bank instruments. Devoid of the option of central bank credit, Member States can solely finance their budget via taxes and financial markets. In reality Member States are extremely dependent on financial markets, since raising taxes is often politically not feasible. Art. 123 TFEU can thus be seen as a disciplining mechanism based on market forces; the assumption being that markets would sanction excessive deficits with higher interest rates. Bond purchases on secondary markets, i.e. bonds which have already been bought by other market participants at market rates, continue to be allowed. Art. 18.1 ESCB Statute even explicitly provides for the instrument. Note, however, that the financing of IMF obligations of Member States (see Chap. 6) by the ECB or NCBs is not regarded as a central bank credit facility and thus allowed under EU law (see Art. 7 Council Regulation (EC) No. 3603/93). Moreover, Art. 124 TFEU ensures the proper functioning of markets and the effectiveness of market forces in relation to EU institutions and Member States by denying them any privileged access to financial institutions (mostly commercial banks), which could otherwise be used to circumvent the rationale of Art. 123 TFEU.[26] Both provisions are further defined in respective regulations: Council Regulation (EC) No. 3603/93 referring to Art. 123 TFEU and Council Regulation (EC) No. 3604/93 dealing with Art. 124 TFEU.[27] When exercising its powers pursuant to Art. 127 TFEU the Eurosystem must also strictly observe the principle of proportionality (Art. 5 (4) TEU).[28]

---

[24]The German Federal Constitutional Court as well as S. Peers define support as the absence of a separate, independent economic policy of the ECB, reference for a preliminary ruling in Gauweiler, 2 BvR 2728/13, para. 39, and Peers (2014).

[25]Lastra (2015, p. 295).

[26]Lastra (2015, p. 295).

[27]OJ 1993 L 332/1 and OJ 1993 L 332/4.

[28]See ECJ, Gauweiler, C-62/14, para. 66 ss.

In terms of procedure, it is the task of the Governing Council to formulate the monetary policy for the Euro area. The adopted measures are subsequently implemented by the Executive Board, which instructs the NCBs (Art. 12.1 ESCB Statute).[29] The Eurosystem's current operational framework consists of the following main instruments for policy implementation:

- Open market operations[30] (Art. 18 ESCB Statute)[31];
- Standing facilities, (Art. 17 ESCB Statute)[32];
- Minimum reserve requirements for credit institutions (Art. 19 ESCB Statute)[33];
- Forward guidance (a communication strategy aimed at directing market expectations).[34]

Generally, the Eurosystem conducts its monetary policy by interacting with financial markets and credit institutions. It does so by buying/selling and lending/borrowing in financial markets as well as providing credit facilities to commercial banks subject to receipt of adequate collateral or security.[35] Through these central bank facilities, which provide the liquidity for the banking sector, the Governing Council sets the key interest rates for the Euro area. Available facilities include the main refinancing operations (MRO) (part of the open market operations, Art. 18.1 s dash ESCB Statute), the deposit facility and the marginal lending facility (both part of the standing facilities). A chronology of adopted measures is regularly published[36] and in the Annex to the ECB's monthly bulletin. Detailed information on the operational framework is contained in the guidelines of the ECB on the implementation of the Eurosystem monetary policy framework.[37]

References

ECB (2011) The Monetary policy of the ECB 2011. https://www.ecb.europa.eu/pub/pdf/other/monetarypolicy2011en.pdf

Herrmann C (2010) Währungshoheit, Währungsverfassung und subjektive Rechte. Mohr Siebeck, Thübingen

Lastra R (2015) International financial and monetary law, 2nd edn. Oxford University Press, Oxford

[29] Proctor (1999, p. 75).

[30] See https://www.ecb.europa.eu/mopo/implement/omo/html/index.en.html.

[31] See also Smits (1997, pp. 264–275).

[32] See also Smits (1997, pp. 260–264).

[33] See also Smits (1997, pp. 275–283).

[34] See Lastra (2015, p. 43 s).

[35] Proctor (1999, p. 76).

[36] See https://www.ecb.europa.eu/press/govcdec/mopo/2016/html/index.en.html.

[37] Available at https://www.ecb.europa.eu/ecb/legal/pdf/oj_jol_2015_091_r_0002_en_txt.pdf.

Murswiek D (2014) ECB, ECJ, Democracy, and the constitutional court. German Law J 15 (2014):147–166
Peers S (2014) Clash of the Judicial Titans: will the Euro survive? EU Law Analysis. http://eulawanalysis.blogspot.de/2014/02/clash-of-judicial-titans-will-euro.html
Proctor C (1999) The Euro and the financial markets, 1st edn. Jordan Publishing Limited, Bristol
Selmayr M (2015) § 23 In: Müller-Graf (ed) Europäisches Wirtschaftsordnungsrecht, Enzyklopädie Europarecht, vol 4. Nomos, Baden-Baden
Smits R (1997) The European Central Bank, institutional aspects, 1st edn. Kluwer Law International, The Hague
Thiele A (2015) Die EZB vor Gericht. ZBB/JBB 2015:295–305
Thiele A (2014) Friendly or unfriendly act? German Law J 15(2014):241–264
Zilioli C, Selmayr M (2001) The law of the European Central Bank, 1st edn. Hart Publishing, Oxford

Chapter 11
Economic Policy Coordination in EMU

> We called economic and monetary union a union that was extremely monetary and scarcely economic.[1]

This statement by *Pascal Lamy*, a former Director General of the WTO and European Commissioner for Trade, captures the asymmetry between monetary and economic integration in EMU nicely. In retrospect, arguably, some of the key policy decisions taken when drafting the treaties or secondary law appear short-sighted or strategically unsound. Similar criticism continues to be voiced over current measures and reforms initiated since the crisis unveiled the flaws of EMU. Nevertheless, such decisions are often rather testimony to (sometimes changing) political realities and convictions than simply to economic necessities. Additionally, matters are made more difficult by the diverse economic landscape of the EU.[2] When examining the economic component of EMU, the term 'economic' refers to budgetary and fiscal policies of Member States. The monetary aspects of the internal market have already been dealt with (Chap. 10); competition Law is not part of this book and the EU budget itself is comparably small in volume and financed completely by "own resources" as opposed to by loans for example (Art. 311 (2) TFEU).[3]

---

[1]Lamy (2012, p. 12).
[2]For the original EMU framework pre-crisis see Amtenbrink and de Haan (2003, p. 1078).
[3]Lastra (2015, p. 291). For more information on the EU's finances see Commission, Where does the money come from?, http://ec.europa.eu/budget/explained/budg_system/financing/fin_en.cfm/other.

C. Herrmann and C. Dornacher, *International and European Monetary Law*,
SpringerBriefs in Law, DOI 10.1007/978-3-319-57642-8_11

11.1 The Case for Economic Policy Coordination in EMU

The key feature of the economic union is that in reality it is not a union (although concrete plans to pursue a genuine economic and monetary union do exist at EU level, see the 'Five Presidents Report'[4] and the Commission's first measures of implementation[5]). Member States retain the main competence for the formulation and execution of economic and fiscal policies (Art. 3 and 4 TFEU which list economic or fiscal policies neither as exclusive nor as shared competences; Art. 2 (3) and 5 TFEU merely speak of "coordination").[6] The notion of an 'asymmetric' EMU, therefore, describes the simultaneous existence of a single (supranational) monetary policy and multiple (national) economic policies.[7] The difficulties of establishing and maintaining a monetary union without a fiscal union were very well known and even officially acknowledged by the *Delors Report.*[8] Both policy areas are deeply intertwined and affect each other in various ways.[9] The convergence criteria are thus supposed to ensure sufficient economic convergence and legal approximation between Member States upon acceding to the monetary union. Once part of the Euro area,[10] a set of primary (Art. 119–126 TFEU), secondary (Stability and Growth Pact, Six-Pack, Two-Pack) and extra-union law (Treaty on Stability, Coordination and Governance) provisions aim to detect, prevent and correct diverging economic developments which could threaten the stability of the Euro area.[11] The ideal of European economic policy is an open market economy with free competition, sustainable public finances and budgetary autonomy of the individual Member State.[12] Nonetheless, as the crisis unfolded, the regulatory framework largely focused on preventive strategies and had few answers or mechanisms to offer for dealing with existing imbalances and negative effects of excessive public debts.[13]

---

[4]Available at https://ec.europa.eu/commission/publications/five-presidents-report-completing-europes-economic-and-monetary-union_en.

[5]See http://europa.eu/rapid/press-release_IP-15-5874_en.htm. On a genuine economic and monetary union see also Lastra (2015, p. 332 s).

[6]On the categories of competence and how Art. 5 TFEU fits in doctrinally see Lastra (2015, p. 292).

[7]Lastra (2015, p. 291).

[8]Committee for the study of EMU, Report on economic and monetary union in the EC, pp. 17 and 19, http://ec.europa.eu/economy_finance/publications/publication6161_en.pdf.

[9]Committee for the study of EMU, Report on economic and monetary union in the EC, p. 17, http://ec.europa.eu/economy_finance/publications/publication6161_en.pdf.

[10]For Member States with a derogation and the status of Denmark and the UK see Art. 139 TFEU, Protocol No. 15 and 16.

[11]Commission, EU economic governance, http://ec.europa.eu/economy_finance/economic_governance/index_en.htm.

[12]Herrmann (2013, p. 29).

[13]Herrmann (2013, p. 29).

11.1.1 Primary Law Foundations of Economic Policy Coordination

The Treaty of Lisbon (effective December 2009), the last comprehensive treaty revision to date, did not substantially alter the legal parameters of EMU. Recent amendments to the framework have been introduced through mainly secondary and extra-union legal acts[14]—a practice which sparked an academic debate on the desirability, long-term consequences and effectiveness of such action.[15] Bear in mind, however, that this form of legal development is not a singularity in the history of European integration. Systematically, the existing primary law provisions can be roughly divided into elements of positive integration, requiring positive action of Member States to coordinate policies and approximate laws,

- Art. 119, 120, 121 TFEU,
  and negative integration, prohibiting certain actions,
- Art. 126 TFEU and to a lesser extent, because they address the ESCB and not Member States, Art. 123, 124 TFEU;
  two provisions do not fit into either of the broad categories since they deal with emergency assistance and liability rules respectively,
- Art. 122 and 125 TFEU.

11.1.1.1 Coordination ('Positive Integration')

The guiding principles and cornerstones for economic policy within the EU and EMU are laid down in Art. 119 and 120 TFEU. Basically, the treaties compel Member States to closely coordinate their economic policies (Art. 119 (1) TFEU), which in turn shall be committed to an open market economy and free competition as well as serve common goals (see Art. 120 TFEU and 3 TEU). When formulating and executing economic policy, Member States need to observe the following principles: stable prices, sound public finances and monetary conditions and a sustainable balance of payments (Art. 119 (3) TFEU).

The purpose of Art. 121 TFEU is to provide a coordination process with procedural and institutional anchors that are indispensable for effective governance. According to said provision, the forum for the coordination process is the Council (Art. 121 (1) TFEU). Coordination is to be achieved through the setting of broad guidelines (Art. 121 (2) TFEU) and its implementation to be controlled by

[14]Lastra (2015, p. 290).

[15]E.g. see Dimopoulos (2014, p. 41 ss).

'multilateral surveillance' (Art. 121 (3) TFEU, a mechanism of peer review).[16] Similarities to IMF law exist here not only with regard to procedure; the content of recommendations made by the Council under Art. 121 (2) TFEU often also resembles that of IMF reports and surveys as well.[17] The Council formulates guidelines for a three year period on the basis of recommendations made by the Commission and in consultation with the European Council. The European Parliament will be informed by the Council but does not take part in the drafting of the recommendation.[18] Furthermore, the Council is competent to adopt recommendations specifically for and confined to the Euro area (the 'outs' are not allowed to vote on such measures, Art. 136 (2) TFEU) as long as they are in line with the overall recommendations issued for the whole EU, Art. 136 (1) in conjunction with Art. 121 (2) TFEU.[19] The performance of the Member States is monitored by the Commission, which reports to the Council. Member States are obliged to assist the Commission by providing all necessary information (Art. 121 (2) TFEU). Based on the Commission's reports, the Council then assesses whether the Member State's economic policies meet the requirements of the guidelines. In the event of a negative assessment, the Commission is entitled to address a warning to the respective Member State (Art. 121 (4) TFEU). The Council on the other hand is able to issue the recommendations necessary to correct the divergence from the guidelines to the Member State concerned (Art. 121 (4) TFEU). Naturally, the Member State in violation of the guidelines is deterred from voting on these recommendations. However, the highest level of escalation foreseen in Art. 121 (4) TFEU is merely the publication of the violation and the necessary recommendations adopted thereupon. Hence, the enforcement of the coordination procedure relies on the peer pressure it potentially exerts. Pursuant to Art. 121 (6) TFEU, a series of regulations and directives have been enacted to provide a more coherent surveillance mechanism and to refine the 'multilateral surveillance' contained in Art. 121 (3) and (4) TFEU (see below).

11.1.1.2 Prohibitions ('Negative Integration')

Sustainable public finances is one of the foundations EMU was and is built on. Germany was a strong proponent of this rule and also the leading architect behind the Stability and Growth Pact (SGP).[20] In contrast to the sometimes rather soft objectives mentioned above, the prohibition of excessive public debt is a firm rule, stipulated in Art. 126 (1) TFEU and further defined in Protocol No 12. Violation of

---

[16] Lastra (2015, p. 293).

[17] Lastra (2015, p. 293).

[18] The current Council recommendation can be found here: http://eur-lex.europa.eu/legal-content/EN/TXT/?uri=OJ%3AJOL_2015_192_R_0009.

[19] The current recommendation for the Member States whose currency is the Euro can be found here: http://ec.europa.eu/europe2020/pdf/csr2015/csr2015_council_euro_en.pdf.

[20] Lastra (2015, p. 288).

this rule triggers the excessive deficit procedure. The procedure's aim is to lead the Member State back onto the path of sustainable finances and therefore the right to sue the offending Member State under Art. 258 or 259 TFEU is suspended for certain stages of the procedure in order not to hamper consolidation efforts. Furthermore, Art. 126 TFEU provides for its own sanction mechanism should Member States persistently fail to comply with the budgetary rules.

The decision whether the size of debt reaches excessive levels is ultimately made by the Council (Art. 126 (6) TFEU). Note that here and during the excessive deficit procedure the Member State allegedly in breach is banned from voting (Art. 126 (13) TFEU). Generally, it is the Council's responsibility to ensure Member States comply with budgetary discipline. Conversely, the continuous, close monitoring of public finances of all Member States as well as the initial assessment on the level of debt is done by the Commission (Art. 126 (2) and (3) TFEU). There is room for discretion when making the assessment (see Art. 126 (2) a) and b) "unless…"; 126 (3) TFEU)), but the reference values are formulated in numerical and quantitative indicators:

- The current or planned deficit (for each budget year) shall not exceed 3% for the ratio of the planned or actual government deficit to gross domestic product at market prices (Art. 1 Protocol No 12);
- The total government debt shall not exceed 60% for the ratio of government debt to gross domestic product at market prices.

Interestingly, the statistical data which informs the decision and is the base for the excessive deficit procedure has to be supplied by the Commission (Art. 4 Protocol No 12) and not the Member States, even though Member States are required to submit relevant information (Art. 3 Protocol No 12). Data collection indeed became problematic as e.g. Greece indicated incorrect data in the past.[21]

Should the Commission conclude that an excessive debt exists or that there is a substantial risk of one, it prepares a report (Art. 126 (3) TFEU). After the Economic and Financial Committee has given its opinion on the report, the Commission addresses an opinion to the Member State and informs the Council accordingly (Art. 126 (4) and (5) TFEU). Thus, the right of initiative in the excessive deficit procedure rests with the Commission.[22] The procedure then follows certain stages and proceeds as follows: The Council determines whether an excessive deficit exists based on the Commission's proposal and statements by the the Member State concerned (Art. 126 (6) TFEU). Depending on the Member State's response there are several escalation levels should an excessive deficit not be remedied. First the Council will make recommendations to the Member State (Art. 126 (7) TFEU), if those remain unasnwered the Council can make them public (Art. 126 (8) TFEU). Further persistence may result in a notification of the Member State by the Council to take the necessary measures within a specified time limit (Art. 126 (9) TFEU). Ultimately

[21]Lastra (2015, p. 299).

[22]ECJ, C-27/04 (Commission v. Council, para. 92).

sanctions (Art. 126 (11) TFEU) can be imposed on the Member State that range from additional information duties when issuing new bonds/securities to fines.

Nonetheless, the prohibition of Art. 126 (1) TFEU and the application of its procedure did not produce the desired results. In fact, unsustainable debt burdens became a crucial issue after 2007 and contributed to the financial crisis' development into the European sovereign debt crisis.[23] A significant loss in the excessive deficit procedure's credibility, caused when Germany (and later France too[24])—the main proponent of stability and budget discipline—violated the budget criteria itself in 2003[25] and by the Council's subsequent omission to take decisive measures despite the Commission's insistence,[26] rendered the mechanism toothless. The 2005 reform of the SGP (see below), which introduced more flexible fiscal rules, completed the picture. The general criticism, leading inter alia to said reform, that purely quantitative criteria are inadequate to assess the sustainability of debt and that greater focus on growth is necessary, predates the German breach and has not per se been proven wrong by the outbreak of the crisis.[27]

The Council is required to abrogate some or all of its decisions or recommendations pursuant to Art. 126 (6)–(11) TFEU to the extent that the Member State has already remedied the situation. Additionally, as soon as the Member State corrects the excessive deficit, the Council is obliged to make a public statement to this effect, provided that a Council recommendation pursuant to Art. 126 (8) TFEU has been published publicly beforehand (Art. 126 (12) TFEU) (i.e. an actus contrarius).

Art. 123 and 124 TFEU (Chap. 10) are often cited alongside Art. 126 TFEU and 125 TFEU as prohibitions. Nevertheless, the systematic classification is misleading, since Art. 123 and 124 TFEU prohibit specific central bank instruments and are directed at the ECB and NCBs. The potential positive effects on public budget discipline are a desired by-product of exposing Member States to market forces, yet do not make the prohibitions primary economic regulations.

11.1.1.3 Emergency Assistance and Liability Clause

Art. 122 TFEU is an expression of the principle of solidarity (Art. 3 (3) TEU) and enables the Council, upon a respective proposal by the Commission, to take appropriate measures (Art. 122 (1) TFEU) or offer financial assistance (Art. 122 (2)

---

[23] Lastra (2015, p. 308).

[24] Council Decision 2003/487/EC of 3 June 2003 on the existence of a government deficit in France, OJ 2003 L 165/29.

[25] Council Decision 2003/89/EC of 21 January 2003 on the existence of a government deficit in Germany, OJ 2003 L 34/16.

[26] For a detailed description of the history of the incident see Lastra (2015, p. 307 s); the principle of equal treatment was also questioned, since the procedure had been strictly applied to Ireland and Portugal before being practically suspended in the cases of Germany and France.

[27] CML Rev. (2004); Lastra (2015, pp. 288 ss and 302 ss). For an overview of ongoing and closed excessive deficit procedures see https://ec.europa.eu/info/node/4287/.

TFEU) in exceptional circumstances.[28] The provision applies to all Member States, but if balance-of-payments difficulties are concerned, Art. 143 and 144 TFEU precede for Member States with a derogation. Art. 122 TFEU is not an exception to Art. 125 TFEU, as their systematic order already demonstrates (exceptions are typically listed after the general rule). Conversely, it shows that the colloquial title given to Art. 125 TFEU 'no-bail-out clause' is a misnomer.[29] There is no absolute prohibition of financial assistance from the EU or other Member States to a Member State in need. Rather, the purpose of Art. 125 TFEU is to remind markets that despite membership in the Euro area each Member State is still "on its own" and requires individual assessment with regard to risk premiums.[30] This falls squarely within the market forces rationale that also inspired other provisions of EMU, e.g. Art. 123, 124 TFEU. Therefore, whereas implicit or explicit guarantees are forbidden, Art. 125 TFEU does not preclude the voluntary supply of financial aid.[31]

11.1.2 Secondary Law

The basic legal skeleton formed by primary law provisions is fleshed out by secondary legislation providing details for economic governance in EMU. The regulatory centrepieces are the Stability and Growth Pact (SGP)[32] and the international law agreement Treaty on Stability, Coordination and Governance (TSCG, often referred to as 'Fiscal Compact'). The Six-Pack and Two-Pack are modifications and reforms of the SGP concluded due to the previous weak effectiveness of the SGP as unveiled by the crisis. The European Semester on the other hand is the title of the annual cycle of economic policy coordination implementation. Its aim is to harmonize the timetables of the various governance tools through synchronisation. The final pillar of economic governance in EMU comprises a soft law agreement (Euro Plus Pact[33]), which is not legally binding nor does it impose sanctions, and the Europe 2020 Strategy, which is a ten year job and growth strategy.

11.1.2.1 The Stability and Growth Pact (SGP)

Most notably, the SGP is not in fact a separate pact or agreement but a package of what was originally a European Council Resolution[34]—representing the political

[28]See also Lastra (2015, p. 296).

[29]Lastra (2015, p. 296).

[30]Smits (1997, p. 77).

[31]ECJ, C-370/12 (Pringle), para. 137.

[32]See https://ec.europa.eu/info/node/4287/.

[33]Gabrisch and Staehr (2014); Lastra (2015, p. 324).

[34]Resolution of the European Council on the Stability and Growth Pact of 17 June 1997, OJ 1997 C 236/1.

commitment to budgetary discipline—and two Council Regulations[35]—strengthening surveillance and coordination (Art. 121 TFEU) as well as speeding up and clarifying the excessive deficit procedure (Art. 126 TFEU). The rules apply to all Member States except for provisions relating to Art. 126 (9) and (11) TFEU, which are solely applicable to Euro area members (Art. 139 (2) TFEU). Despite the rationale behind the SGP—to tighten the rules on fiscal discipline—it had little influence on the fiscal behaviour of Member States.[36] Breaches were a common feature in the life of the pact and after the Commission's unsuccessful attempts to discipline Germany and France it was further watered down through a reform in 2005.[37]

Regarding content, the SGP comprises a preventive and a corrective arm relating to Art. 121 and 126 TFEU respectively. Council Regulation 1466/1997 as amended by Council Regulation 1055/2005 dealt with the multilateral surveillance (prevention) and mainly subjected Member States to elaborate duties of information supply (annual stability ("Ins") and convergence ("Outs") programs).[38] But it also foresaw an 'early warning procedure' in case the fiscal situation of a Member State began to deteriorate (Art. 6 (2) Council Regulation 1466/1997). The heart of the original SGP was Council Regulation 1467/1997 as amended by Council Regulation 1056/2005. The regulation fills the procedural frame prescribed by Art. 126 TFEU with specific rules and provides a system of sanctions in order to penalize Member States in breach. The rigidity of the rules was relaxed in 2005. Furthermore, qualitative considerations (the general economic atmosphere, efforts towards 'good' causes, i.e. international solidarity) were introduced to supplement the overall rather quantitative approach of Art. 126 TFEU and Protocol No. 12.

11.1.2.2 Six-Pack and Two-Pack

The secondary legislative acts that became known under the names Six- and Two-Pack constitute reforms of the SGP as the latter proved 'weak' in the course of the crisis. The Six-Pack (2011) comprises five regulations and one directive.[39] Further amendments are contained in the two regulations of the Two-Pack (2013).[40]

In summary, the Six-Pack amends the SGP in all its elements and introduces a new surveillance tool: The macroeconomic imbalance procedure (MIP).[41] Key points of SGP improvement include: To enhance the incentive generated by the

---

[35]Council Regulation (EC) No 1466/1997, OJ 1997 L 209/1; Council Regulation (EC) No 1467/1997, OJ 1997 L 209/6.

[36]For a more detailed history of the SGP see Lastra (2015, p. 302 ss).

[37]For a detailed analysis of the breaches that occurred see Lastra (2006, p. 265 ss).

[38]Lastra (2015, p. 305 s).

[39]All six are published in OJ 2011 L 306/1 ss.

[40]Both published in OJ 2013 L 140/1 ss.

[41]The MIP was introduced by the Regulations 1174/2011 and 1176/2011; see also https://ec.europa.eu/info/node/4320/.

'medium-term objective' (MTO). The medium-term objective varies but always aims for a structural balance of the budget. The surveillance of progress in this area is now embedded into a broader assessment that is restrictive in nature, yet takes into account various variables relevant to short- and medium-term budget developments, e.g. structural reforms, impacts of uncontrollable, unusual events.[42] Moreover, the corrective arm was revised with a view to the operationalization of the debt criterion (i.e. the 60% threshold), which is now on equal footing with the 3% deficit criterion. Additionally, the initiation of the excessive deficit procedure is now associated with a requirement to set up a fiscal and economic partnership program. Such programs will most likely contain similar measures as those taken under EU/IMF adjustment programs.[43] Directive 2011/85/EU addresses the negative experiences with incorrect data supply by Member States and sets minimum formal standards for budgetary frameworks. Lastly, the voting procedure within the excessive deficit procedure was altered into a reversed qualified majority voting system with the effect that the Commission can now essentially force the Council to act. It can do so by resubmitting a recommendation, which will be deemed to be adopted unless the Council rejects it within 10 days by a qualified majority.[44] The Two-Pack regulations focus on Euro area Member States and aim to strengthen fiscal surveillance specifically in the Euro area. This includes a special surveillance regime for Euro area Members which requested financial assistance from the European emergency funds (Greece, Ireland, Spain, Portugal, Cyprus).[45]

11.1.3 Extra-Union Law Measures

Due to the lack of suitable legal bases and/or political hurdles in the prescribed legislative or amendment procedures, Member States reverted to extra-union legal measures. These are quite simply international law agreements on an intergovernmental basis. Despite their formal legal separation and independence, these measures often foresee the involvement of EU institutions for implementation purposes and are applied and interpreted in accordance with EU law. In the current context, the Treaty on Stability, Coordination and Governance is an example of this practice.

11.1.3.1 TSCG

The TSCG (often referred to as 'Fiscal Compact') is an agreement between all EU Member States except for the UK, Czech Republic and Croatia. It entered into force

[42]Lastra (2015, p. 315).
[43]Lastra (2015, p. 318).
[44]Art. 4 (2), 5 (2) and 6 (2) Regulation 1173/2011.
[45]Lastra (2015, p. 317).

on 1 January 2013 and seeks to strengthen fiscal discipline in the euro area through a balanced budget rule and an automatic correction mechanism. In a nutshell, the TSCG covers three main areas [(1) fiscal stability; (2) economic coordination and (3) governance of the Euro area], repeating and reinforcing some of the EU law provisions but also introducing new rules to the existing elaborate framework.

References

Amtenbrink F, de Haan J (2003) Economic governance in the EU: Fiscal policy discipline versus flexibility. CML Rev 40:1075–1106

Dimopoulos A (2014) The use of international law as a tool for strengthening economic governance in the EU and its implications on EU Institutional integrity. In: Adams M, Fabbrini F, Larouche P (eds) The constitutionalisation of EU budgetary constraints. Hart Publishing, Oxford, pp 41–63

Gabrisch H, Staehr K (2014) The Euro plus pact. ECB Working Paper Series No 1650/2014. https://www.ecb.europa.eu/pub/pdf/scpwps/ecbwp1650.pdf

Herrmann C (2013) Legal aspects of the European sovereign debt crisis. Hitotsubashi J Law Polit 41:25–40

Lamy P (2012) Pourquoi l'euro? Regards croisés sur l'économie 11:12–22

Lastra R (2006) Legal foundations of international monetary stability. Oxford University Press, Oxford

Lastra R (2015) International financial and monetary law, 2nd edn. Oxford University Press, Oxford

Rev CML (2004) Editorial comments: whither the stability and growth pact? CML Rev. 41:899–907

Smits R (1997) The European Central Bank, institutional aspects, 1st edn. Kluwer Law International, The Hague

Chapter 12
The External Relations of EMU

"Who is 'Mr. Euro'?"[1]

The Euro area is not a separate and closed system, but operates on an international scale beyond the borders of its Member States' territory (cf. Art. 63 TFEU, Member States' membership and participation in international organisations and fora, e.g. IMF, OECD, G7 and G10). As Member States transferred significant parts of their monetary sovereignty[2] to the EU,[3] internal (see Chaps. 9 and 10) and external competences (see below) had to be allocated accordingly. In addition to the determination of exchange-rate and control regimes, the ability to influence the international development of the financial architecture is of paramount importance in an economically globalized world. Furthermore, relations to third countries or international organisations are vital for the Euro's role as an international currency and for the EU's integration project as a whole.[4] Therefore, to ask, who is 'Mr. Euro', means to ask, who represents the Euro area externally and with whom does the political responsibility for the external relations of the currency union reside?

12.1 The Acting Institutions/Entities

First of all, the active participation in international relations, i.e. the capacity to create rights and obligations under international law, requires international legal personality.[5] This immediately disqualifies the Euro area, the Eurogroup, the

[1]See Lastra (2015, p. 342).
[2]Only very limited residual elements of monetary sovereignty remain at Member State level, i.e. coinage, legislation against counterfeiting and falsification.
[3]Herrmann (2002, p. 10).
[4]Herrmann (2002, p. 1), Zilioli and Selmayr (2001, p. 171 s).
[5]Zilioli and Selmayr (2001, p. 172).

C. Herrmann and C. Dornacher, *International and European Monetary Law*,
SpringerBriefs in Law, DOI 10.1007/978-3-319-57642-8_12

Eurosystem and the ESCB from formally acting on behalf of EMU externally. Potential actors on the international stage therefore are:

- The EU (cf. Art. 47 TEU),
- the Member States,
- the ECB (cf. Art. 282 (3) TFEU) and
- the NCBs.[6]

12.1.1 The Division of Competence

The treaty provisions dealing with the external relations of EMU are Art. 138, 219, 127 (2) TFEU and Art. 6.1, 6.2, 12.5, 22, 23, 30.5 and 31.1 ESCB Statute. Generally, the external competences are divided between the Council (main role) and the ECB (secondary role). Member States, on the other hand, retain a residual external competence (Art. 219 (4) TFEU), which mostly refers to economic matters and instances where international law prevents EU institutions from exercising their external competence (see below). Since NCBs are national agencies and simultaneously 'an integral part of the ESCB' (Art. 14.3 ESCB Statute), they remain competent to act externally in areas which are not ESCB tasks (Art. 6.1, 14.4 ESCB Statute), subject to the respective national law, of course. Additionally, they may—subject to the ECB's approval—continue to participate in international monetary institutions, e.g. the Bank for International Settlements (BIS), Art. 6.2 ESCB Statute. Naturally, NCBs of Member States whose currency is not the Euro are exempted from these rules, notwithstanding their participation in the ESCB (Art. 42.1 ESCB Statute).

The arrangement reflects the norm in many countries where the more strategic choices such as the exchange-rate and exchange-rate regime are attributed to political authorities (usually Ministry of Finance, in case of the EU the Council) and the operational issues are left to central banks.[7] Nevertheless, the division of competence may have adverse effects if policy actions are not being coordinated. Notably, this is due to the causal link between exchange-rates and monetary policy,[8] but also because multiple players add layers of complexity to any given field. A viable solution embodied in Art. 138 and 219 TFEU is the involvement of the ECB in the decision-making procedure of the Council, albeit one of limited scale (see below).

[6] Zilioli and Selmayr (2001, p. 173).

[7] Lastra (2015, p. 340).

[8] For a detailed study of the policy interplay see Gianviti (2014, p. 545 ss).

12.1.2 *The Doctrine of Parallelism*

The ECJ developed the doctrine of parallelism in the *ERTA* case.[9] The doctrine is based on the theory of implied powers and essentially stipulates that external competences can be derived not only from express Treaty provisions but also from existing internal competences (i.e. implied by the existence of an internal competence). The rationale behind the doctrine is to avoid divergence of external and internal competences, which might undermine or circumvent the latter.[10] Since the doctrine fills a legal loophole, its scope is restricted to cases where no explicit competences exist.[11] In conclusion, external EMU competences are therefore primarily determined by the provisions enumerated above and only supplemented by implied powers in case of a divergence of internal and external competences.

12.1.3 *Judicial Review*

Noteworthy in this context is furthermore that the express derogation from Art. 218 TFEU in Art. 219 (1) and (3) TFEU does not extend to Art. 218 (11) TFEU, which remains applicable for agreements pursuant to Art. 219 TFEU.[12] This conclusion is based on the general principle that the scope of a derogation is strictly limited to its content. Art. 218 (11) TFEU provides for ex ante judicial review of international law agreements (i.e. exchange-rate system agreements) in the form of an ECJ opinion issued prior to their entry into force. A negative opinion suspends the entry into force until the agreement is amended or the Treaties revised accordingly. Some commentators support an extensive reading of the provision and grant the ECB legal standing under Art. 218 (11) TFEU in order to protect its prerogatives despite a clear wording to the contrary.[13]

12.2 Exchange-Rate Policy of EMU

The exchange-rate policy of the EMU is governed by Art. 219 TFEU with operational aspects dealt with by Art. 127 (2) TFEU and Art. 23 ESCB Statute. The former provision depicts different kinds of regulatory approaches to establishing an exchange-rate regime. Note, however, that it only refers to monetary relations with non-EU Member States ('true external aspects of EMU') and does not constitute a

[9]ECJ, ERTA (Commission v Council), C-22/70.

[10]Lastra (2015, p. 345).

[11]Herrmann (2002, p. 6).

[12]Herrmann (2002, p. 12).

[13]Herrmann (2002, p. 12).

legal base for arrangements with Member States with a derogation. This reading is further supported by the repositioning of the provisions (Art. 219 (1)–(4) TFEU), which were formerly included in Art. 111 (1)–(3) and (5) TEC in the chapter on monetary policy,[14] but can now be found in the chapter on international agreements. Meanwhile, Art. 127 (2), 282 (1) TFEU entrust the Eurosystem with certain operational tasks related to exchange-rate policy. The Eurosystem acts through the Governing Council of the ECB (Art. 6.1, 12.5 ESCB Statute).

12.2.1 Objective of Exchange-Rate Policy

Regardless of the split competence between internal monetary policy (Eurosystem) and external exchange-rate regime (Council), both policy areas are committed to the primary objective of price stability (Art. 119 (2) TFEU). Interestingly, the Treaties do not make any reference to exchange-rate stability. From a legal point of view, exchange-rate stability is therefore a negligible objective as long as volatile exchange-rates are not negatively affecting price stability that is.[15]

12.2.2 Formal Exchange-Rate Arrangements (Art. 219 (1) TFEU)

The formal exchange-rate agreement addressed in Art. 219 (1) TFEU is not intended to introduce a new category of international agreements but rather refers to exchange-rate regime agreements of the Bretton Woods (see Chap. 2) type.[16] Other (less formal) agreements fall under either Art. 219 (2) or (3) TFEU.

The responsibility for the negotiation and conclusion of such agreements lies with the Council.[17] Regarding the prescribed procedure, the structure of the provision is rather convoluted: Rules on the initiation and conduct of negotiations of formal agreements are contained in Art. 219 (3) TFEU. Conversely, the procedural requirements for the conclusion of said agreements are laid down in Art. 219 (1) TFEU. Hence, the procedure is as follows: Negotiations and the modalities thereof can be arranged by the Council (for example the Council can entrust another EU institution or Member State to conduct the negotiations on behalf of the union), deciding by a qualified majority (Art. 16 (3) TFEU), upon recommendation of the Commission and after consulting the ECB. Art. 135 TFEU allows the Council to

---

[14]Art. 111 TEC did, however, also not apply to Member States with a derogation despite its systematic position in the Treaty framework, see Herrmann (2002, p. 11).

[15]Lastra (2015, p. 341).

[16]Smits (1997, p. 380), Herrmann (2002, p. 11).

[17]Lastra (2015, p. 346).

request a recommendation of the Commission. The Council is not bound by a recommendation, yet it is a formal prerequisite for the initiation of negotiations.

If the negotiations are successful, the Council can conclude the agreement by unanimous act pursuant to another recommendation from either the ECB or the Commission and after consulting the ECB, in an endeavor to reach a consensus consistent with the objective of price stability, as well as the European Parliament (Art. 219 (1) TFEU). However, the consensus is not a prerequisite for the conclusion of an agreement. In case of an insoluble dispute the final word belongs to the Council.[18] It is these intricacies that make the Council at least formally the main protagonist in external monetary relations. Any agreement concluded under this provision is legally binding on all EU institutions (including the ECB) and all Euro area Member States. Within such an exchange-rate system it is again the Council's task to adopt, adjust or abandon central rates of the Euro subject to the procedure outlined above (minus the negotiation part), except that the European Parliament is not consulted but only informed thereof.

12.2.3 Floating Exchange-Rates (Art. 219 (2) TFEU)

The Euro is a freely floating currency (cf. Art. IV Sec. 2 IMF Articles of Agreement). In practice, no use has ever been made of the option provided in Art. 219 (1) TFEU. This allows the Council to influence exchange-rate policy by formulating 'general orientations' (Art. 219 (2) TFEU) instead of entering into formal exchange-rate arrangements. These orientations must be without prejudice to the primary objective of price stability and are required to be abstract ('general') in content.[19] Specific interferences with concrete operations of the ECB are therefore not permitted under Art. 219 (2) TFEU. Whether or not these orientations would exert binding force on the ECB when conducting foreign exchange operations is subject to legal debate.[20] However, since a non-binding nature would render the provision meaningless, it is suggested that the ECB would indeed be bound by general orientations issued by the Council provided they are not compromising the price stability objective. Moreover, this view is supported by the wording of Art. 127 (2) second indent TFEU ["(…) consistent with the provisions of Art. 219"].

The procedure deviates slightly from the one foreseen in Art. 219 (1) TFEU. General orientations are adopted by the Council with a qualified majority (cf. Art. 16 (3) TEU) upon recommendation of either the Commission (after consulting the ECB) or of the ECB. No information or consultation of the European Parliament is required. Again, the Council has yet to avail itself of this option. According to the Resolution of the European Council on economic policy coordination in Stage III of

---

[18]Herrmann (2002, p. 11).

[19]Herrmann (2002, p. 11 s).

[20]Against a binding nature: Smits (1997, p. 399); in favor: Herrmann (2002, p. 12).

EMU and on Art. 109 and 109b of the EC Treaty from 1997 the Council shall only adopt general orientations in ‘exceptional circumstances’ and generally regard exchange-rates ‘as the outcome of all other economic policies’. Furthermore, the Resolution gives a nod to the independence of the ECB and cautions the Council to respect it should there ever be the need to adopt a general orientation. Consequently, in practice it is the ECB that is operationally responsible for the exchange-rate policy of EMU under the current regulatory framework.[21]

12.2.4 Agreements Concerning Monetary or Foreign Exchange Regime Matters (Art. 219 (3) TFEU)

There is some controversy about the nature of Art. 219 (3) TFEU. Commentators are divided on whether the provision is merely a procedural one or also contains further explicit external competences for the Union.[22] Due to the wording, which is formulated in broader terms than Art. 219 (1) TFEU (the latter only regulates a specific kind of agreement), it is possible to perceive Art. 219 (3) as a general competence for the conclusion of international agreements in monetary matters despite its systematic position towards the end of the provision. The competence includes instances where third countries wish to adopt the monetary regime of the Euro, i.e. Euroization or currency board arrangements, and request the approval of the Union (for examples see Chap. 9). Other examples that fall under Art. 219 (3) TFEU are informal or less formal international law agreements concerning the exchange-rate regime of the Euro.

12.2.5 Tasks of the ECB (Art. 127 (2) TFEU)

It has already been mentioned above that, in practice, the ECB operates the management of the exchange-rate due to the lack of any formal agreement or general orientations by the Council. The legal base for this operational function in exchange-rate matters is contained in Art. 127 (2) TFEU and Art. 22, 23 ESCB Statute. The competences listed in Art. 22 and 23 ESCB Statute go beyond mere exchange-rate policy and include international central bank coordination (e.g. participation in the Bank for International Settlements, BIS) as well as the promotion of the smooth operation of payment systems. The latter is actually an example for the application of the doctrine of parallelism, as Art. 22 ESCB Statute does not confer an explicit external competence yet such can be implied from the existence of the internal competence. Any decision in the area of external ECB

[21]Lastra (2015, p. 347).

[22]Lastra (2015, p. 346).

competences is made by the Governing Council of the ECB (Art. 6.1, 12.5 ESCB Statute). For more information on its decision-making procedure see Chap. 8.

12.3 International Relations of EMU

Notwithstanding the recent crisis and regulatory shortcomings of EMU, the Euro as a currency has quickly developed into an international and reserve currency, second probably only to the US Dollar, since its introduction in 1999.[23] With a view to this role, Art. 138 TFEU determines that the Council shall decide on issues of particular relevance for EMU's external representation, particularly to ensure common positions within the respective international organisation or forum. Finding a common position is especially important in areas where the EU has an exclusive competence yet international law prevents it from seizing its external competences. A notable example is the IMF, which only permits nation states as members.[24] Apart from potential decisions under Art. 138 TFEU, which allows for the formulation of concrete positions, Member States are generally obliged not to act contrary to the goals and interests of the Union (duty of cooperation, cf. Art. 4 (3) TEU).[25]

Regarding procedure, Art. 138 TFEU does not hold any surprises. The Council takes the appropriate decisions by qualified majority pursuant to a respective proposal by the Commission and after consulting the ECB. A current example is a Commission proposal for the progressive establishment of a unified representation of the Euro area in the IMF.[26] According to the Commission's vision, the Euro area would be represented at ministerial level by the President of the Eurogroup and in the Executive Board by a Director of a Euro area constituency. The proposal is related to the Five Presidents Report which ultimately aims to establish a genuine Economic and Monetary Union. A unified external representation is only one element thereof.

In summary, there is no Mr. Euro. Representational tasks are divided among several institutions and players with varying degrees of influence (Council, ECB, Commission, Member States, NCBs). From an international law perspective it is, however, the Council that possesses most of the fundamental decision-making powers of a monetary sovereign (conclusion of formal/informal exchange-rate arrangements, determining the central rate for the Euro within formal agreements, restricting capital and payments mobility).

---

[23]For a detailed analysis of the international role of the Euro see ECB (2015).

[24]This is in contrast to the EU's membership in the WTO, see https://www.wto.org/english/thewto_e/countries_e/european_communities_e.htm.

[25]See also ECJ opinion 2/91, para. 36.

[26]Commission proposal COM (2015) 603, http://eur-lex.europa.eu/legal-content/EN/TXT/?uri=CELEX%3A52015PC0603.

References

ECB (2015) The international role of the Euro. https://www.ecb.europa.eu/pub/pdf/other/euro-international-role-201507.en.pdf

Gianviti F (2014) Relationship between monetary policy and exchange-rate policy. In: Cottier T, Lastra R, Tietje C, Satragno L (eds) The rule of law in monetary affairs. Cambridge University Press, Cambridge, pp 545–569

Herrmann C (2002) Monetary sovereignty over the euro and external relations of the euro area: competence, procedures and practice. Eur Foreign Aff Rev 7:1–24

Lastra R (2015) International financial and monetary law, 2nd edn. Oxford University Press, Oxford

Smits R (1997) The European central bank, Institutional aspects. Kluwer Law International, The Hague

Zilioli C, Selmayr M (2001) The law of the European central bank. Hart Publishing, Oxford

Chapter 13
EMU and the Sovereign Debt Crisis—Legal Aspects of Financial Assistance for Member States

13.1 Evolution of a Crisis

The narrative of a financial crisis is a peculiar thing. One may deduct from the term crisis that something unforeseeable is happening, something out of the ordinary, perhaps even unprecedented. However, history provides us with many examples of the seemingly 'extraordinary'.[1] The patterns are often comparable and unfold in similar ways: From a new opportunity to generate profit, brought about by a cesura (e.g. new technology, new inventions, surprising success, beginning or end of a war) that suddenly alters investment behavior; followed by a 'boom', which is fueled by 'herd behavior' and 'euphoria' of investors; to the moment the specific market peaks and the first investors begin to cash-out their profits and withdraw their investments. At this point, others may or may not follow the signal, it may or may not cause a 'crash' or 'run'. The outcome depends on various variables such as market developments, the regulatory framework in place as well as the policy response of public authorities.[2] While each crisis has its own roots and causes, the above outline proved to be an accurate template for the '2007/2008 global financial crisis', which quickly developed into a fiscal crisis in Europe. But how exactly did an American/Anglo-Saxon financial crisis turn into a European sovereign debt crisis of this magnitude?[3] The question arises particularly because the overall debt burden of the Euro area increased much less during the acute years of the financial crisis (2008–2011) than those of the USA or Japan for instance.[4]

---

[1]Generally see Kindleberger (2005), Reinhard and Rogoff (2011).
[2]See Lastra (2015, p. 149 ss).
[3]The European sovereign debt crisis is often falsely referred to as Euro crisis despite there being no currency crisis.
[4]ECB (2012, p. 57).

C. Herrmann and C. Dornacher, *International and European Monetary Law*, SpringerBriefs in Law, DOI 10.1007/978-3-319-57642-8_13

What brought Europe into crisis mode, however, was the rather tragic interplay of dysfunctional markets, fiscal irresponsibility, macroeconomic imbalances and the legal framework of EMU, revealing the debt burden of certain Member States to be unsustainable. Despite Greece not being the first EU Member State to face difficulties after the subprime mortgage bubble burst in the USA, it is common understanding that the autumn of 2009, when the newly elected Greek Government had to admit their budget deficit was double the size than previously notified (12.5% of GDP instead of 6% of GDP, triple of the allowed 3%), marks the start of the European sovereign debt crisis.[5] Yet, the underlying causes for the crisis date back a lot further. There was Greece, of course, which falsified its data in order to meet the convergence criteria and enter the Euro area prematurely. There was Ireland on the one hand, whose massively expanding banking sector became extremely exposed to external risks,[6] and countries like Portugal and Spain on the other hand, whose macroeconomic imbalances turned into a liability despite initially sound public finances.[7] Further contributing factors included the almost consistent disregard among Member States for the rules set out in the Stability and Growth Pact to an extent that breaches became the norm rather than the exception. The latter was significantly aided by financial markets, which did not adequately sanction the fiscal irresponsibility of individual Member States despite signs to the contrary, hence giving an incentive to indebtedness by providing cheap capital. And then there was and is EMU itself, which established a monetary union without a fiscal union, whose legal framework contains detailed (unfortunately often neglected) rules on preventive measures and policies (cf. Art. 123–126 TFEU), but is largely silent on remedies for times in which that preventive mechanism fails and which renders its Member States very dependent on financial markets in the absence of monetary financing and devoid of a national currency they can control.[8] Last but not least, the "state-bank-nexus" of modern day economies. States and their national banking sector form a community of fate, forged by mutual dependencies. While national banks and financial institutions are normally the principal customers for government bonds, their States of origin are usually the only ones willing and capable to provide liquidity or equity in times of a bottleneck.

Therefore, once the subprime mortgage bubble burst in the USA, a chain reaction was set in motion due to the global interconnectedness of economies and financial markets. Many States, including Euro area Member States, had to intervene and assist their national banks in order to prevent a collapse of the whole sector. Simultaneously, large stimulus packages were necessary to absorb at least the worst consequences of the ensuing recession and set new positive impulses. Naturally, all of these measures required enormous funds, which Member States

---

[5]Herrmann (2013, p. 26).

[6]Lastra (2015, p. 309).

[7]Lastra (2015, p. 313).

[8]Their situation essentially compares to countries whose debt is denominated in foreign currency.

had to procure somewhere.[9] A recourse to monetary instruments (e.g. devaluation of their currency, inflation policies) in order to obtain a competitive advantage or to reduce the net value of the nominal debt burden was not an option for Euro area Member States. In conclusion, the effects of the global financial crisis (recession and imminent bank bankruptcies) called for high public expenditure, which caused markets to reevaluate the creditworthiness of Member States and increase interest rates to the extent that some peripheral Euro area Member States were on the verge of losing access to financial markets. The by then apparent possibility of a sovereign default in one's own currency significantly weakened market confidence in the general stability of the Euro. More critically, however, it confirmed fears of contagion with the budgetary difficulties making inroads from peripheral Euro area Member States to those at the very center.

In their attempt to overcome the crisis and simultaneously strengthen EMU with a view to future developments ('learning the lesson' of the sovereign debt crisis), the Member States and the EU devised a threefold approach: (1) Safeguarding the solvency of Member States; (2) reforming the legal framework with regard to economic coordination and particularly fiscal discipline and (3) the establishment of a Banking Union. The following analysis will focus on measures providing financial aid. Measures of the ECB as well as the establishment of a Banking Union will be addressed separately, as their objectives differ from those of financial assistance granted within the context of the crisis (Chap. 14). Generally, the ECB is concerned with the monetary fallout of the debt crises and the consequences thereof for the single monetary policy and currency. Conversely, the reforms of the legal framework have already been pointed out in the chapters dealing with the respective subject matters (e.g. Chap. 11).

13.2 Measures of Member States

The measures taken by Member States can be classified as measures based on extra-union law (i.e. international law agreements) and measures based on union law (i.e. measures adopted according to provisions in the Treaties).

13.2.1 Measures Based on Extra-Union Law

13.2.1.1 Bilateral Loans

Once it became clear that Greece needed external support to cope with its budgetary meltdown the other Euro area Member States decided to prevent the looming

[9]Between 2008 and 2012, the Commission approved public subsidies of 5058.9 bn. Euros in total for the 'bail-out' of banks and financial institutions, see Selmayr (2015, §23, para. 57).

payment default by providing bilateral loans to Greece on May 2nd 2010. It seemed the only option at the time for want of any other available instrument or legal rules in the Treaties on how to proceed in such a situation. The loan package of overall 110 bn. Euros consisted of 80 bn. Euros from Member States and 30 bn. Euros from the IMF. The loans were pooled centrally by the Commission.[10] The loan-share of each creditor Member State was proportionate to their respective capital subscription to the ECB. A major condition for the provision of financial aid was budget consolidation. Similarly to the IMF's approach, the loans were disbursed in installments over three years instead of in one lump sum and continuation thereof was subject to compliance with the conditions (strict conditionality). For the purpose of performance surveillance, the so-called 'Troika' (staff members of the Commission, ECB and IMF) was established and later on officially renamed 'the Institutions' for the sake of Greece's sensitivities.

Through this first 'Greek loan facility' (GLF)[11] 73.8 bn. Euros were disbursed—52.9 bn. from Member States and 20.9 bn. from IMF funds. Unfortunately, the financial problems of Greece proved to be more severe than initially anticipated. Contributing factors in this regard were the ensuing recession after the crisis as well as the effects of the austerity policy (loan conditions). As the readjustment of the financial terms of the facility (e.g. extension of the final maturity, reduction of the margin) turned out to be insufficient, the remaining 37 bn. of the first GLF were transferred to a second economic adjustment program and topped up (by the EFSF, see below). Furthermore, the Greek debt was restructured in spring 2012 by private creditors foregoing 53.5% of the nominal value of the Greek bonds they were holding. The transaction affected bonds worth 199 bn. Euros in total.[12,13]

13.2.1.2 European Financial Stability Facility (EFSF)

As outlined above, other peripheral countries such as Portugal and Spain began to face similar problems as Greece. Fearing a domino effect, serious doubts about the general financial stability in the EU spread rapidly among financial market participants.[14] In order to counter the hysteria, remedy the contagion and rebuild market confidence in the Euro area the European Council decided to set up a

[10]Commission (2015, p. 12).

[11]Commission (2015, p. 12).

[12]For a detailed analysis see Zettelmeyer et al. (2013).

[13]Commission, Post-Programme Surveillance for Ireland, http://ec.europa.eu/economy_finance/assistance_eu_ms/ireland/index_en.htm.

[14]Herrmann (2013, p. 30).

so-called ‘rescue umbrella’ in May 2010.[15] It was supposed to provide up to 750 bn. Euros for financial aid and it features three different instruments: The European Financial Stabilization Mechanism (EFSM, see below), the European Financial Stability Facility (EFSF)[16] and IMF facilities. The EFSF is a company registered in Luxembourg and established under Luxembourg private law.[17] It is owned by Euro area Member States.[18] Despite the unique legal set up and rather complex legal framework, its operating principle is quite simple: The EFSF can raise money on financial markets by issuing marketable instruments and subsequently lend the procured funds to its shareholders—the Member States. The EFSF’s effective lending capacity of 440 bn. Euros and market activity is covered by guarantees of Euro area Member States (worth almost 780 bn. Euros), whose respective volume is determined by each Member State’s capital share of the ECB. However, loans to Member States in distress (Art. 2 (1) a) EFSF Framework Agreement) is not the only tool available to the EFSF, albeit the most significant one. Further optional measures include precautionary credit lines, facilities for the re-capitalization of financial institutions (Art. 2 (1) c) EFSF Framework Agreement) and bond purchases on primary and secondary markets (Art. 2 (1) b) EFSF Framework Agreement) in order to avoid contagion. During the life of the EFSF, the loan commitment summed up to 198.2 bn. Euros in total, of which 184.6 bn. Euros were actually disbursed.[19]

Regarding the complex legal framework, the EFSF is essentially governed by the Articles of Association and the more important Framework Agreement between the shareholders (Euro area Member States) of the EFSF. Moreover, the Board of Directors, the general decision-making body of the EFSF, governs all financial instruments with the exception of loans through guidelines. Each Euro area Member State is represented in the Board. Due to its temporary nature (cf. Art. 2 (11) EFSF Framework Agreement) the EFSF ceased to exist on June 30th 2013. More precisely, its statutory activity ended and thus it may no longer engage in new financing programs. Nonetheless, it continues to exist for the purpose of loan repayment by debtor Member States. Apart from this residual function, its other former rights and obligations were transferred to the newly created European Stability Mechanism (ESM), which has taken over the exercise of these rights and obligations (Art. 13 (10) EFSF Framework Agreement).

---

[15] European Council, Document No. 9596/10, http://data.consilium.europa.eu/doc/document/ST-9596-2010-INIT/en/pdf.

[16] See https://www.esm.europa.eu/efsf-overview.

[17] Commission (2015, p. 12).

[18] Its 17 shareholders are: Austria, Belgium, Cyprus, Estonia, Finland, France, Germany, Greece, Ireland, Italy, Luxembourg, Malta, Netherlands, Portugal, Slovakia, Slovenia and Spain, see EFSF, key facts, http://www.efsf.europa.eu/about/key-figures/index.htm.

[19] German Federal Ministry of Finance, European financial assistance: EFSF and EFSM, http://www.bundesfinanzministerium.de/Content/EN/Standardartikel/Topics/Europe/european-financial-assistance-efsf-efsm.html#doc13020bodyText2.

13.2.1.3 European Stability Mechanism (ESM)

The ESM is the indirect successor of the EFSF.[20] The rationale behind the creation of yet another mechanism was the slow realization among Member States that temporary or ad hoc measures would suffice neither to regain market confidence nor to successfully end the continuing crisis. Therefore, a permanent crisis resolution mechanism for the Euro area was established on 8 October 2012 (after a partially problematic ratification process, e.g. in Germany[21]): The European Stability Mechanism.[22] The ESM enjoys quite a few similarities with the EFSF mostly with regard to design and structure, but also exhibits significant differences in terms of the legal construction. While the EFSF was created under Luxembourg private law as a special purpose vehicle, the ESM is an international institution with legal personality under international law. The ESM possesses a capital stock of around 704.8 bn. Euros, following the most recent accessions [Latvia (2014) and Lithuania (2015)]. In contrast to the EFSF, whose activities were merely guaranteed by Member States' governments, the ESM's capital is divided into 80.5 bn. of paid-in capital and around 624.3 bn. Euros of callable capital. Once again, individual subscriptions are proportionate to each Member State's capital share of the ECB.[23] Financial aid is provided in accordance with the purpose of the ESM to safeguard the financial stability of the Euro area as well as of its Member States and subject to strict conditionality (cf. Art. 12 (1) ESM Treaty). The ESM's toolbox (Art. 14–18 ESM Treaty) resembles the one of the EFSF with instruments for the provision of financial assistance ranging from precautionary conditioned credit lines to bond purchases on the primary and secondary market. Nevertheless, loans remain the standard instrument, as they can also be granted for the re-capitalization of financial institutions. Procedural requirements on the other hand are contained in Art. 13 ESM Treaty. Perhaps most importantly from a constitutional point of view are the ESM's close relations with EU institutions and the IMF. The collaboration is reflected in several procedural steps, where the Commission or the ECB for example are entrusted with decisive assessment tasks (cf. Art. 13 (1) ESM Treaty).

Since it began its work in October 2012, the ESM approved financial assistance for Cyprus (9 bn. Euros),[24] Spain (100 bn. Euros)[25] and Greece (86 bn. Euros).[26] Cyprus and Spain only called up 6.3 and 41.3 bn. Euros respectively and were able

---

[20]See https://www.esm.europa.eu/.

[21]See BVerfG, Judgment of 18 March 2014—2 BvR 1390/12.

[22]For a detailed analysis see Ohler (2011, p. 47 ss).

[23]German Federal Ministry of Finance, European Financial Assistance: ESM, http://www.bundesfinanzministerium.de/Content/EN/Standardartikel/Topics/Europe/european-financial-assistance-esm.html.

[24]See https://www.esm.europa.eu/assistance/cyprus.

[25]See https://www.esm.europa.eu/assistance/spain.

[26]See https://www.esm.europa.eu/assistance/Greece.

to conclude the program earlier than expected, whereas Greece entered a three year program in August 2015 and thus far has received a cumulative amount of 31.7 bn. Euros.

13.2.2 Measures Based on EU Law

The incomplete legal framework of EMU largely focused on prevention but did not include any rules on how to ensure the solvency of Euro area Member States, debt restructuring, procedures for a sovereign default or exit of the Euro area. Only selectively and confined to specific, narrow issues do the Treaties offer remedies: Medium term assistance for balance-of-payments difficulties of non-Euro area Member States (Art. 143 and 144 TFEU) and Emergency Liquidity Assistance (ELA) by NCBs for temporarily illiquid, but solvent financial institutions (based on Art. 14.4 ESCB Statute). Therefore, just one of the measures taken to assist Euro area Member States in distress and to avoid a sovereign default or the disintegration of the Euro area as a whole was based on EU law.

13.2.2.1 European Financial Stabilization Mechanism (EFSM)

The EFSM is one of the pillars of the 2010 'rescue umbrella' and it can provide up to 60 bn. Euros in financial assistance. The legal foundation for the mechanism is Council Regulation (EU) No. 407/2010,[27] which in turn was based on Art. 122 (2) TFEU. Essentially, it empowers the Council to instruct the Commission (Art. 3 Regulation (EU) No. 407/2010) to provide loans or credit lines for Member States which are facing severe economic or financial difficulties or are threatened thereof due to exceptional occurrences beyond their control (Art. 2 (1) and recital (1) Regulation (EU) No. 407/2010). An example of exceptional circumstances would be the serious deterioration of the international economic and financial environment.[28] The funds for this particular financial aid are raised on financial markets or borrowed from financial institutions by the Commission on behalf of the EU (Art. 2 (1) Regulation (EU) No. 407/2010). Consequently, it is the EU budget that backs up the entire borrowing/lending activity of the EFSM.[29] The continued provision of funds is subject to compliance with economic or financial adjustment programs as agreed in the Memorandum of Understanding (MoU) between the Commission and the beneficiary Member State (Art. 3 (4) b) Regulation (EU) No. 407/2010). To this end, the performance of the beneficiary Member State is monitored by the Commission in consultation with the ECB. Surveillance does

[27]OJ 2010 L 118/1.

[28]See Commission (2015, p. 5).

[29]See Commission (2015, p. 5).

factor in the general economic environment as well. Furthermore, the Commission together with the ECB can assess whether further financial assistance is needed and suggest adjustments of the conditions if they deem it necessary (Art. 3 (7) Regulation (EU) No. 407/2010). The final decision is a prerogative of the Council, which may adopt the Commission proposal by a qualified majority.

Beneficiaries initially included only Ireland (22.5 bn. Euros) and Portugal (24.3 bn. Euros). Both programs were concluded in 2014. A more recent example of EFSM financial assistance is Greece, which received short-term assistance (a bridge loan) in July 2015 of 7.16 bn. Euros.[30]

13.3 Legal Assessment

Each of the measures outlined above was accompanied by intense public scrutiny and controversial legal debate. Considering the incomplete and fragmented legal framework of EMU in this context the controversy does not come as a surprise. Generally, the debate centered around two main issues: (1) Does EU law allow the 'rescue' of Member States in financial difficulties at all and (2) are the regulatory choices legal/valid under EU law. Doubts about the general possibility of financial assistance beyond the selective and few express provisions contained in the Treaties were mostly founded in Art. 125 (1) TFEU—the so called 'no bail-out clause' (see Chap. 11). Especially among German scholars the provision was often read as an absolute prohibition of any kind of financial aid due to the purpose and rationale of the rule.[31] Yet, this understanding of the prohibition disregards the objectives set out in Art. 3 (3) TEU and the solidarity principle expressed therein. Moreover, each of the abovementioned measures (GLF, EFSF, EFSM, ESM) constitutes new and voluntarily provided facilities as opposed to assuming existing liabilities of other Member States. In this respect 'no bail-out clause' is a misnomer as it suggests that even voluntary assistance would be prohibited. However, wording, purpose and context of the provision rather indicate that only specific forms of assistance (e.g. automatic guarantees for future liabilities or assumption of existing ones) are not allowed, since they are regarded to be particularly dangerous for the stability of the common currency and the budgetary discipline of Member States. The ECJ followed the same reasoning in its *Pringle* judgement and stipulated that Art. 125 (1) TFEU does not prevent Member States from granting each other financial assistance as long as such practices do not undermine budgetary discipline.[32] Meanwhile, as far as the ESM is concerned this is now—albeit only in a declaratory manner—expressly regulated in Art. 136 (3) TFEU.

---

[30]Commission, EFSM, http://ec.europa.eu/economy_finance/eu_borrower/efsm/index_en.htm.

[31]See e.g. Ruffert (2011, p. 1785), Palmstorfer (2012, p. 775 ss).

[32]ECJ, Pringle C-370/12, para. 137; Merino (2012, p. 1627).

Incidentally, neither Art. 123 TFEU (prohibition of monetary financing) nor Art. 127 TFEU in conjunction with Art. 3 (1) (c) TFEU (the exclusive monetary policy mandate of the Eurosystem) are convincing arguments against the principal legality of inter-Member State financial assistance. While the former represents a substantive rule, which limits the operational options of Central Banks and thus is only directed at the ECB and NCBs,[33] the latter also does not affect the Member States' ability to create extra-union mechanisms under international law in the area of economic or fiscal policy.[34] Bear in mind that the principle of conferral does not apply to the sovereign Member States. They are only restricted in areas where competences have been transferred to the EU, but otherwise remain competent to act internationally. Notwithstanding their legal capacity though, the development has caused some concerns among commentators and scholars, which perceived the solution of union problems by extra-union measures as critical.[35] The resurgence of intergovernmentalism, they fear, may lead to a significant fragmentation of EU law.

Further criticism was raised against the EFSM. The allegation was that the Regulation (EU) No. 407/2010 generally classifies financial crises as extraordinary occurrences calling for emergency assistance. Indeed, such a standardization would contradict the exceptional nature of Art. 122 (2) TFEU. However, the regulation does not contain an automatism of this kind. Conversely, each provision of financial aid requires an in-depth assessment of the individual case of the applicant by the Commission in consultation with the ECB and is ultimately decided by the Council. The regulation merely provides a general procedural framework, not a general determination of the subject matter at hand. A related issue concerns the procurement of funds. Art. 122 (2) TFEU does not contain any specifications in this regard. Yet, considering that any kind of financial aid normally needs to be refinanced, Art. 122 (2) TFEU can reasonably be read as an implied authorization of refinancing operations for the emergency assistance.

Another joint allegation against ESM, EFSM and EFSF was that it would violate Art. 124 TFEU. The argument is based on an understanding of ESM, EFSM and EFSF to be functionally equivalent to financial institutions. Two points may be worth discussing in this regard. First none of the above mechanisms currently has access to central bank financing as normal financial institutions do.[36] Thus the specific hazardous situation Art. 124 TFEU aims to prevent does not arise here. Furthermore, Member States do not receive privileged access by virtue of their sovereign power (i.e. abusing their power to get better conditions other market participants cannot get), they are rather the beneficiaries of mechanisms over whose work they do not have control in the sense that they cannot force the assistance.

---

[33] ECJ, Pringle C-370/12, para. 125.

[34] ECJ, Pringle C-370/12, para. 93.

[35] See Scicluna (2012, p. 489 ss), Hinarejos (2015, pp. 85–100), Tuori and Tuori (2014, p. 216 ss).

[36] For the possibility of central bank access for the ESM see ECB, Opinion (CON/2011/24), Recital No. 9, OJ C 140/8, http://eur-lex.europa.eu/legal-content/EN/TXT/?uri=uriserv:OJ.C_.2011.140.01.0008.01.ENG&toc=OJ:C:2011:140:TOC.

Therefore, with a view to its scope and purpose, the more convincing arguments speak in favor of the ESM, EFSM and EFSF being compatible with Art. 124 TFEU.

In summary, one can conclude that none of the above discussed measures by the Member States violated EU law. Hence, the future of the Euro and the Euro area (at least the financial and economic stability aspects thereof) will continue to be safeguarded by the ESM and the EFSM.

References

Commission (2015) Report on the borrowing and lending activities of the EU in 2015, COM 375 final. https://ec.europa.eu/transparency/regdoc/rep/1/2015/EN/1-2015-327-EN-F1-1.PDF

ECB (2012) Analysing government debt sustainability in the Euro area. ECB Mon Bull 55–69. https://www.ecb.europa.eu/pub/pdf/other/art1_mb201204en_pp55-69en.pdf

Herrmann C (2013) Legal aspects of the European sovereign debt crisis. Hitotsubashi J Law Polit 41:25–40

Hinarejos A (2015) The Euro area crisis in constitutional perspective. Oxford University Press, Oxford

Kindleberger C (2005) Manias, panics and crashes. A history of financial crises, 5th edn. John Wiley & Sons, Hoboken

Lastra R (2015) International financial and monetary law, 2nd edn. Oxford University Press, Oxford

Merino A (2012) Legal developments in the economic and monetary union during the debt crisis: the mechanisms of financial assistance. CML Rev 49:1613–1645

Ohler C (2011) The European stability mechanism: the long road to financial stability in the Euro area. In: Giegerich T, Odendahl K, Matz-Lück N (eds) German yearbook of international law 2011, vol 54. Duncker Humblot, Berlin, pp 47–74

Palmstorfer R (2012) To bail out or not to bail out? ELRev 37:771–784

Reinhard C, Rogoff K (2011) This time is different. Princeton University Press, Princeton (reprint)

Ruffert M (2011) The European debt crisis and european union law. CML Rev 48:1777–1805

Scicluna N (2012) EU constitutionalism in flux: is the Euro area crisis precipitating centralisation or diffusion? Eur Law J 18:489–503

Selmayr M (2015) § 23. In: Müller-Graf (ed) Europäisches Wirtschaftsordnungsrecht, Enzyklopädie Europarecht, vol 4. Nomos, Baden-Baden

Tuori K, Tuori K, (2014) The Euro area crisis: a constitutional analysis. Cambridge University Press, Cambridge

Zettelmeyer J, Trebesch C, Gulati M (2013) The Greek debt restructuring: an autopsy. economic policy 2013. http://scholarship.law.duke.edu/cgi/viewcontent.cgi?article=5343&context=faculty_scholarship

Chapter 14
EMU and the Sovereign Debt Crisis—Legal Aspects of Monetary Policy Responses and the Banking Union

14.1 The Monetary Policy Reactions to the Crisis

In 2008/2009 the Eurosystem acted promptly and efficiently in responding to the crisis by supplying markets with sufficient amounts of central bank money in order to preempt illiquidity problems.[1] Keeping the monetary circulation going and transmission mechanisms functioning is vital for a central bank (see Chap. 10) and the initial efforts of the Eurosystem were indeed effective in averting dramatic contractions and alleviating the condition of financial markets. Of course, this was before 2009/2010 when the crisis picked up speed in Europe and the first phase of the sovereign debt crisis was heralded in. With it came the times of 'non-standard' monetary policy measures, as the ECB classifies them (see below).[2] However, the policy shift was less pronounced than it may seem. Technically, it was simply an expansion of the central bank's toolbox (cf. Art. 18.1 as well as Art. 20.1 ESCB Statute). The Eurosystem continues to employ traditional monetary policy instruments, e.g. setting the key interest rates and reserve requirements, in response to the crisis and to conduct monetary policy.[3] Notwithstanding the importance and role of 'standard' monetary policy instruments, the following discussion will focus on ECB decisions that caused controversy among economic and legal experts alike. One can therefore distinguish between standard (less controversial, see Chap. 10) and non-standard measures (more controversial, see below).

---

[1]ECB (2009, p. 9 s).

[2]Note that the classification is a factual, not a legal one. Art. 18.1 ESCB Statute does not distinguish between standard and non-standard measures. Other commentators referred to these measures as unconventional, see Lastra (2015, p. 41); C. Villalón, opinion of advocate general in Gauweiler, C-62/14, para. 100.

[3]Lastra (2015, p. 257). For an overview of the development of key interest rates see https://www.ecb.europa.eu/stats/policy_and_exchange_rates/key_ecb_interest_rates/html/index.en.html.

C. Herrmann and C. Dornacher, *International and European Monetary Law*,
SpringerBriefs in Law, DOI 10.1007/978-3-319-57642-8_14

14.2 Non-standard Monetary Policy Measures

The factual distinction between standard and non-standard measures is not necessarily based on the specific instrument used—although the choice of instrument clearly is an indication—but rather depends on key features of each measure (volume, conditions, precedence, timing etc.). One reason for the increasingly blurred lines between standard and non-standard is that even standard monetary policy instruments, e.g. the setting of interest rates, were used in a non-standard fashion during this crisis.[4] However, the ECB's (non-standard) crisis response so far mainly comprised the following: (1) enhanced credit support for financial institutions; (2) the relaxation of collateral requirements in its lending operations ('qualitative easing') and (3) structural open market operations.

14.2.1 Enhanced Credit Support

The provision of enhanced credit support was facilitated through the introduction of long-term refinancing operations (LTRO)[5] and targeted long-term refinancing operations (TLTRO).[6,7] Essentially, LTROs and TLTROs are intended to supplement the standard main refinancing operations (MRO), which normally have a maturity of just one week, by offering longer-term funding (maturity of 3–48 months). The addition allows for a more refined provision of liquidity especially in times of crisis and it may also serve other monetary policy objectives due to its length (e.g. strengthening monetary transmission channels or countering deflation). TLTROs for example, specifically target to ease private sector credit conditions and stimulate bank lending to the real economy.[8] They do so by linking the amount that banks can borrow to their lending activity vis-á-vis non-financial corporations and households. A further sign of the current accommodative monetary policy focus of the ECB is the full allotment strategy often included in the terms and conditions of these operations. Full allotment thereby means that banks will receive as much liquidity as they request, always provided, of course, that they are offering sufficient collateral for the requested amount.[9] Despite its popularity among financial institutions and the undoubtedly needed liquidity stimulus in order to unlock the

---

[4]See ECB (2014).

[5]ECB (2011b).

[6]ECB, Targeted longer-term refinancing operations (TLTROs), https://www.ecb.europa.eu/mopo/implement/omo/tltro/html/index.en.html.

[7]Generally see Lastra (2015, p. 261).

[8]Hence the name "targeted long-term refinancing operations" as opposed to the non-targeted "long-term refinancing operations.

[9]Deutsche Bundesbank, Glossary—Full allotment, https://www.bundesbank.de/Navigation/EN/Service/Glossary/Functions/glossary.html?lv2=128958&lv3=145730.

paralyzed interbank financing, a product of the global financial crisis, the enhanced credit support faced criticism. Some commentators question the contribution of LTROs and TLTROs to the real economy.[10] Others point out that these measures reinforce rather than mitigate the vicious link between States and banks, because many banks invested the additional liquidity in sovereign bonds.[11]

14.2.2 Qualitative Easing

The enhanced credit support was complemented by a simultaneous relaxation of collateral requirements (qualitative easing). Generally, banks and other financial institutions can only borrow from the Eurosystem, if they provide sufficient collateral (Art. 18.1 ESCB Statute).[12] The aim of this concept of adequate collateral is to protect the Eurosystem from incurring losses in its lending activity. On the other hand this also requires sufficient collateral being available to a broad range of counterparties for the necessary liquidity provision to function smoothly within the euro area. Which assets are eligible as collateral is defined in the "Standard Eurosystem Collateral Framework", whose main part is an ECB guideline, and in the "Temporary Framework", which consists mostly of ECB decisions.[13] Eligible assets fulfill certain criteria, specified in the framework (e.g. Art. 62 ss. ECB Guideline (EU) 2015/510). If necessary, the collateral requirements can therefore be relaxed or tightened by adjusting the criteria accordingly.[14]

14.2.3 Structural Open Market Operations

Even though MROs, LTROs and TLTROs also belong to the group of open market operations, it makes sense to distinguish these from the outright purchases presented below as the latter are employed to "adjust the structural position of the Eurosystem vis-à-vis the financial sector".[15] These measures therefore pursue more strategic monetary policy goals as opposed to primarily an adequate liquidity supply for banks and financial institutions.

---

[10]Lastra and Louis (2013, 57 ff).

[11]Lastra (2015, p. 261).

[12]See also ECB, Collateral, https://www.ecb.europa.eu/paym/coll/html/index.en.html.

[13]The documents are available at https://www.ecb.europa.eu/ecb/legal/1002/1014/html/index-tabs.en.html#tf.

[14]For an historic overview of the adjustments made to the collateral framework of the Eurosystem during the crisis years see https://www.ecb.europa.eu/pub/pdf/mobu/mb201307en.pdf.

[15]ECB, The Eurosystem's instruments, https://www.ecb.europa.eu/mopo/implement/html/index.en.html.

14.2.3.1 Asset Purchase Programmes

The Eurosystem currently employs three asset purchase programmes—the covered bond purchase programme (CBPP3),[16] the asset-backed securities purchase programme (ABSPP)[17] and the public sector asset purchase programme (PSPP, see below)—and has recently added a fourth one: the corporate sector purchase programme (CSPP).[18] All programmes include outright purchases of assets, but differ in terms of eligible asset types as well as in which markets the purchases are being made. Consequently, primary market purchases are only foreseen for assets issued by private entities in accordance with Art. 123 TFEU. This kind of purchase activity of the Eurosystem is commonly referred to as "quantitative easing" (QE) and is not to be confused with the other purchase programmes separate and independent thereof: SMP and OMT.

14.2.3.2 The Securities Market Programme

On 14 May 2010, the ECB introduced the Securities Market Programme (SMP).[19] The SMP is a bond purchase programme with the option to hold these until maturity for (1) marketable debt instruments on secondary markets issued by Euro area Member States and (2) on primary and secondary markets for instruments issued by private entities incorporated in the Euro area. The programme constitutes an open market operation which falls under Art. 18.1 ESCB Statute. It was characterized by the ECB as a non-standard measure aimed at addressing the malfunctioning of security markets and restoring an appropriate monetary policy transmission mechanism. Following severe tensions in several financial markets,[20] the ECB had concluded that these tensions were hampering "*the monetary policy transmission mechanism and thereby the effective conduct of monetary policy oriented towards price stability in the medium term*".[21] The temporary programme was active from May 2010 until September 2012 when the last purchases under the SMP were made. During this time, the Eurosystem purchased bonds of Ireland (14.2 bn.), Greece (33.9 bn.), Spain (44.3 bn.), Italy (102.8 bn.) and Portugal (22.8 bn.) amounting to a total of 218 bn. Euros.[22] Today (April 2017), the remaining

---

[16]OJ 2014 L 335/22.

[17]Decision of the ECB of 19 November 2014 (ECB/2014/45), OJ 2015 L 1, p. 4.

[18]See https://www.ecb.europa.eu/press/pr/date/2016/html/pr160421_1.en.html.

[19]Decision of the ECB of 14 May 2010 (2010/281/EU), OJ 2010 No L 124, p. 8, http://eur-lex.europa.eu/legal-content/EN/TXT/?uri=uriserv:OJ.L_.2010.124.01.0008.01.ENG&toc=OJ:L:2010:124:TOC.

[20]See ECB (2011a, p. 47 ss).

[21]2nd Recital Decision of the ECB of 14 May 2010 (2010/281/EU), OJ 2010 No L 124, p. 8.

[22]ECB (2013).

securities held by the Eurosystem under the SMP portfolio amount to 100 bn. Euros[23] and they will be held until maturity.[24] The design, purpose and implementation of the programme set it apart from large-scale asset purchase programmes (often referred to as quantitative easing, see below) that are usually employed to expand the monetary base. In fact, the ECB actually ensured the absorption of any additional liquidity generated by the SMP purchases through weekly liquidity-absorbing operations until June 2014.[25] This provides further evidence that the programme is not concerned with quantitative easing. With regard to effectiveness, commentators observed that the intervention overall succeeded in reducing yields and volatility of government bond markets.[26]

14.2.3.3 The Outright Monetary Transactions Programme

The SMP was de facto terminated when the Governing Council of the ECB decided to launch another open market operation programme on 6 September 2012: the Outright Monetary Transaction Programme (OMT).[27] OMT foresees the ex-ante unlimited purchase of debt instruments in the secondary government bond market. Respective purchases would be conditional upon the issuing Member State taking part in an ESM macroeconomic adjustment or precautionary programme. Other features of the programme include the focus on bonds with a maturity between one and three years, no preferred creditor status for the ECB and full sterilization of the additional liquidity generated. However, the legal acts necessary to fully establish the programme were never adopted nor was OMT ever implemented. There was no need to do so; the mere announcement via the ECB press release proved sufficient to influence market participants accordingly. OMT is yet another example of monetary policy being conducted through guiding expectations (expectation channel). Its purpose was and is—the required legal acts can be adopted at any time if the ECB deems it necessary—to safeguard an appropriate monetary policy transmission and the singleness of the monetary policy. According to the ECB, unfounded fears among market participants about the reversibility of the Euro were causing severe distortions in government bond markets as evidenced by widening spreads in interest rates for short-term sovereign debt among Member States.[28] In particular, the distortions kept interfering with the transmission of monetary policy measures, e.g. lowering of central rates proved to have little to none effect in some

---

[23]ECB, Open Market Operations, https://www.ecb.europa.eu/mopo/implement/omo/html/index.en.html.

[24]ECB, Terminated programmes, https://www.ecb.europa.eu/mopo/implement/omt/html/index.en.html.

[25]ECB (2012b, p. 30).

[26]Ghysels et al. (2014, p. 1).

[27]ECB (2012c).

[28]ECB (2012a, p. 7).

Member States' markets while others continued to respond appropriately. Hence, the singleness of monetary policy or more specifically the consistent effectiveness of monetary policy across the union was in danger.

14.2.3.4 Quantitative Easing

QE refers to the secondary market's public sector asset purchase programme (PSPP)[29] that supplements or extends already existing purchase programmes, notably the CBPP3 and the ABSPP (see above). The envisaged average volume of all programmes combined is now 60 bn. (originally 60 bn., from April 2016 through March 2017: 80 bn.) Euros[30] per month across the Euro area with purchases to continue at least until December 2017.[31] The expansion of the asset purchase programmes is a direct response of the Eurosystem to the lasting deflationary tendencies within the Euro area and an attempt to re-approximate the inflation rate to the targeted 2%. Ultimately, QE illustrates the Eurosystem's attempt to provide monetary stimulus to the real economy in times of the ECB's key interest rates already being at a record low and failing to produce said stimulus.

14.3 Legal Assessment

It goes without saying that the ECB—just as any other EU institution—is subject to judicial review (cf. Art. 35 ESCB Statute) and therefore must abide by the rule of law. Courts on the other hand must respect the ECB's margin of discretion when conducting monetary policy,[32] which is mainly derived from the principle of central bank independence (Art. 130 TFEU) as well as the special expertise of the body as acknowledged in several provisions of primary EU law (cf. Art. 20 ESCB Statute). Even though previous lawsuits against ECB decisions were unsuccessful before the European General Court (EGC)—one being inadmissible[33] another found to be unjustified[34]—'savers' and other opponents of the ECB's current monetary policy eventually found their way to the ECJ when the German Federal Constitutional Court (GFCC) made its first (and only) preliminary reference (under Art. 267 (1) TFEU) to date. The decision was a controversial one under German constitutional

[29]ECB, Decision (ECB/2015/10), OJ L 121/20.

[30]ECB, Asset purchase programmes, https://www.ecb.europa.eu/mopo/implement/omt/html/index.en.html.

[31]ECB (2015); ECB, Asset purchase programmes, https://www.ecb.europa.eu/mopo/implement/omt/html/index.en.html.

[32]EGC, Judgement of 7.10.2015, (Accorinti and others/ECB) T-79/13, para. 68.

[33]EGC, Order of 10.12.2013, (von Storch and others/ECB) T-492/12; the case was appealed to the ECJ, see C-64/14 P, who dismissed the appeal as unfounded.

[34]EGC, Judgement of 7.10.2015, (Accorinti and others/ECB) T-79/13.

law and of course also from a wider European perspective.[35] While the majority seemed to welcome the GFCC's willingness to finally ask the ECJ for guidance in EU law matters, there was a common feeling that this may not have been the ideal case to do so. Nevertheless, the reference raised several legal issues about the OMT (and indirectly the SMP). Most notably, the ECB allegedly acted beyond the scope of its mandate (Art. 127 (1) TFEU) and violated Art. 123 (1) TFEU by circumventing the prohibition of primary market government bond purchases with functionally equivalent (and explicitly allowed, cf. Art. 18.1 ESCB Statute) secondary market government bond purchases. The cumulative reasons cited for this read of the programmes were: (1) The aim to reduce interest rates for certain government bonds; (2) the selectivity of OMT; (3) the conditionality link to ESM programmes; (4) the possibility to hold bonds until maturity; (5) the ECB forgoing a preferred creditor status; (6) the increased risk of losses; (7) the interference with the free formation of market prices for bonds and (8) the incentive for market participants to purchase bonds on primary markets.

Regarding the distinction between monetary policy and economic policy, the definition the ECJ reverted to has already been discussed in Chaps. 9 and 10. Essentially, the mere fact that the SMP, OMT or even QE have effects on economic or fiscal policy areas is not sufficient to alter the nature of the measure. Provided that the objective of the instrument is a monetary one and that the principle of proportionality (Art. 5 (4) TEU) is being observed, beneficial or adverse side-effects for Member States are no deterrent.

As far as Art. 123 (1) TFEU is concerned, the objections (4), (5) and (6) are the least convincing, since Art. 18.1 ESCB Statute explicitly allows the holding of bonds until maturity. The risk of losses as well as a preferred creditor status are mentioned nowhere in the treaties and are not part of the prohibition. Particularly, the risk of losses typically comes along with investments of this kind and is usually taken into account when assessing interest rates. The selectivity on the other hand is testimony to the fragmented territory and financial markets of EMU—there are simply no Eurobonds for the Euro area—as well as to the very reason for the intervention: the disruption of monetary transmission mechanisms in only some Member States. The same medicine for all only works if all face similar issues. Moreover, the conditionality link to ESM programmes may very well be justified under Art. 127 (1) TFEU as support of general economic policies of Member States as long as it does not interfere with price stability. This is where the sterilization practice of the ECB becomes a crucial factor. In the current deflationary environment, however, not only would it be unnecessary but rather counterproductive for price stability purposes. Hence the discontinuation of sterilization operations in relation to the SMP portfolio in June 2014. Conversely, the objections (1), (7) and (8) may be able to substantiate a circumvention of Art. 123 TFEU if these reasons lead to an abrogation of the sanctioning effects of (primary) market forces. However, since the ECB never intended to reveal in advance when, how much and

[35]See German Law Journal—Special Issue Vol. 15, March 2015.

at what price it was willing to buy, the formation of a market price remains possible and so are sanctions via market forces. Overall, neither of the measures constitutes a circumvention of Art. 123 (1) TFEU.

In the case of QE, the monetary policy objective is much more obvious and should be less controversial despite the considerable volume of the purchase programme. So far, the purchasing activity of the Eurosystem also has not hampered the formation of a market price in primary markets. Thus, QE does not circumvent Art. 123 (1) TFEU either.

Some commentators voiced fears that the bond purchase programmes are really cross Member State financing through the backdoor ("transfer union"), which would violate Art. 125 TFEU. The logic behind this allegation is that if these purchases inflict large losses upon the Eurosystem, the Member States may be forced to recapitalize the NCBs and ultimately the ECB. However, this scenario is highly hypothetical and too remote to justify the assumption that the ECB is establishing a prohibited fiscal transfer union within the Euro area.

In conclusion, the Eurosystem has managed to steer the Euro relatively stable through troubled times and received legal backing from the ECJ, which ascertained the legality of SMP and OMT under EU law in the *Gauweiler* case.[36]

14.4 Banking Union

Last but not least, the newly established so-called banking union.[37] The banking union is not per se a measure to counter the existing crisis, but represents a way to move forward. It is a reform of the legal framework of EMU, designed to prevent a future crisis of this kind. While other reforms focused on the behavior of Member States, this particular one addresses the financial sector. In Chap. 13 the roots of the crisis were discussed and among others the asymmetry of EMU as well as the state-bank community of fate were accounted for facilitating the development. With a view to remedy some of these causes and based on the realization that a single market for financial services needs a single supervision of financial institutions, the banking union was established.[38] The union is framed by two pillars: A Single Supervisory Mechanism (SSM) and a Single Resolution Mechanism (SRM). The core novelty is basically the centralization of financial supervision tasks at the ECB's Supervisory Board. In the wake of Five Presidents Report the Commission proposed a third pillar to be established through a regulation:[39] A European Deposit Insurance

[36]ECJ, Gauweiler, C-62/14, http://curia.europa.eu/juris/document/document.jsf;jsessionid=9ea7d2dc30d5c6ac2019ec4a427db3e1ec35c8202caa.e34KaxiLc3qMb40Rch0SaxuSbx90?text=&docid=165057&pageIndex=0&doclang=EN&mode=lst&dir=&occ=first&part=1&cid=958335.

[37]See https://www.bankingsupervision.europa.eu/about/bankingunion/html/index.en.html.

[38]Lastra (2015, p. 357 ss).

[39]Commission, proposal for a regulation of the European Parliament and of the Council, COM (2015) 586 final, http://eur-lex.europa.eu/legal-content/EN/TXT/?uri=CELEX:52015PC0586.

Scheme (EDIS)[40] in order to complete and strengthen the Banking Union. EDIS would gradually assume the function of national Deposit Guarantee Schemes (DGS) and thereby ultimately lead to a mutualization of saving guarantees.

The SSM is based on Council regulation (EU) No 1024/2013[41] (SSM Regulation) and became operative on 4 November 2014. Subsequently, another regulation (EU) No 468/2014,[42] this time of the ECB, was added to regulate the cooperation between the ECB and the competent national supervisory authorities. The latter was necessary since the ECB is only directly responsible for the supervision of 'significant' institutions whereas less significant institutions remain under the supervision of national authorities. Similar to the ESCB, the idea is that national authorities work closely together within an integrated system under the lead of the ECB. The SSM applies to all Euro area Member States and to those non-Member States that opt to join the SSM. Overall, approximately 6000 banks across Europe are currently covered by the SSM.[43] A logical counterpart of the SSM is the SRM. The SRM refers to crisis management and applies to all banks covered by the SSM. Its purpose is to establish common rules and procedures for the resolution of failing banks with a view to incur minimal costs for taxpayers and the real economy.[44] The legal basis of the mechanism are a Council regulation (EU) No 806/2014,[45] a Bank Recovery and Resolution Directive and an Intergovernmental Agreement between the participating Member States on the transfer and mutualization of contributions into the Single Resolution Fund (SRF).[46]

References

ECB (2009) Governing council decisions on non-standard measures, ECB Monthly Bulletin June 2009. https://www.ecb.europa.eu/mopo/decisions/html/mb200906_pp9_10.pdf?80bfeddc5f38b8e989780f9a5f32755f

ECB (2011a) Monthly Bulletin September 2011. https://www.ecb.europa.eu/pub/pdf/other/box5_mb201109en.pdf?4ea5db0a28b79140f1f3075a20c39919

ECB (2011b) Press Release of 08.12.2011, ECB announces measures to support bank lending and money market activity. https://www.ecb.europa.eu/press/pr/date/2011/html/pr111208_1.en.html

ECB (2012a) Monthly Bulletin September 2012. https://www.ecb.europa.eu/pub/pdf/mobu/mb201209en.pdf

[40]See https://ec.europa.eu/info/business-economy-euro/banking-and-finance/banking-union_en.

[41]OJ L 287/63.

[42]OJ L 141/1.

[43]Commission, Banking Union, http://ec.europa.eu/finance/general-policy/banking-union/index_en.htm.

[44]Lastra (2015, p. 366).

[45]OJ L 225/1-90.

[46]For the legislative history of the SRM see Commission, SRM, http://ec.europa.eu/finance/general-policy/banking-union/single-resolution-mechanism/index_en.htm.

ECB (2012b) Monthly Bulletin January 2012. https://www.ecb.europa.eu/mopo/pdf/mb201201en_box4.pdf?a10f1009db1b231f1f9b10c0159637f7
ECB (2012c) Press Release of 06.09.2012, Technical Features of Outright Monetary Transactions. http://www.ecb.europa.eu/press/pr/date/2012/html/pr120906_1.en.html
ECB (2013) Press Release of 21.02.2013, Details on securities holdings acquired under the Securities Markets Programme. https://www.ecb.europa.eu/press/pr/date/2013/html/pr130221_1.en.html
ECB (2014) Press Release of 05.06.2014, ECB introduces a negative deposit facility interest rate. https://www.ecb.europa.eu/press/pr/date/2014/html/pr140605_3.en.html
ECB (2015) Press Release 22.01.2015, ECB announces expanded asset purchase Programme. https://www.ecb.europa.eu/press/pr/date/2015/html/pr150122_1.en.html
Ghysels E, Idier J, Manganelli S, Vergote O (2014) A high frequency assessment of the ECB Securities Markets Programme. ECB Working Paper Series No 1642. https://www.ecb.europa.eu/pub/pdf/scpwps/ecbwp1642.pdf?1bdb15cbcae0548d98610f8e020f7b5c
Lastra R (2015) International financial and monetary law, 2nd edn. Oxford University Press, Oxford
Lastra R, Louis J-V (2013) EMU: history, trends and prospects. Yearb. Eur. Law 32:57–206

FSC
www.fsc.org
MIX
Papier | Fördert
gute Waldnutzung
FSC® C083411

Kolibri 360 GmbH
Ferdinand-Jühlke-Straße 7
99095 Erfurt, Deutschland
produktsicherheit@kolibri360.de